# The Woman Writer

## THE HISTORY OF THE SOCIETY OF WOMEN WRITERS & JOURNALISTS

D1362841

ESSEX CC LIBRARIES

30130 165470799

# The Woman Writer

## THE HISTORY OF THE SOCIETY OF WOMEN WRITERS & JOURNALISTS

SYLVIA KENT

The History Press

*Love to Peter, Sally and Jennifer for their support.*

First published 2009

The History Press
The Mill, Brimscombe Port
Stroud, Gloucestershire, GL5 2QG
www.thehistorypress.co.uk

© Sylvia Kent, 2009

The right of Sylvia Kent to be identified as the Author
of this work has been asserted in accordance with the
Copyrights, Designs and Patents Act 1988.

All rights reserved. No part of this book may be reprinted
or reproduced or utilised in any form or by any electronic,
mechanical or other means, now known or hereafter invented,
including photocopying and recording, or in any information
storage or retrieval system, without the permission in writing
from the Publishers.
British Library Cataloguing in Publication Data.
A catalogue record for this book is available from the British Library.

ISBN 978 0 7524 5159 6

Typesetting and origination by The History Press
Printed in Great Britain

# Contents

# Acknowledgements

My special thanks to Valerie Dunmore, Frances Clamp, Jean Bowden, Pat Alderman, Jean Morris and Jean Marian Stevens for their time and support. Thanks also to Dame Frances Campbell-Preston, Lady Susan Hussey, Janie Hampton, Verily Anderson and Elizabeth Hart. Appreciation to Nigel Roche, librarian at St Bride Library, London; the British Museum Library; the London Library; the Women's Library; Chris Brewster of the Cater Museum; Stationers' Hall archivist; the London Press Club; *The Lady* staff, the archivist at *The Stage*; Dr Carl Spadoni at McMaster University Library, Ontario; the archivist at Lucy Cavendish College, Cambridge University, and the archivist at Swanwick Summer School.

Every effort has been made to trace ownership of photographs and to check that the facts given in this book are correct. Unless otherwise stated, all illustrations come from the archives of the Society of Women Writers & Journalists. My apologies for any unwitting errors or omissions.

# Introduction

Since its creation on 1 May 1894, the Society has attracted the company of many of the world's most famous women writers, journalists, poets, playwrights and associated creative people involved in the wider world of literature, film, music, theatre and entertainment.

Sadly, space constraints do not allow inclusion of every member. However, as the Society is expanding year by year and with such a long and fascinating history, it was felt important for posterity that as much as possible be recorded in one place.

This is an important year in the annals of the Society. Although Centenary celebrations took place with great gusto in 1994, 2010 is special, as it marks the centenary of the birth of one of our most notable Presidents – Joyce Grenfell.

Joyce often said that she loved being our President. Although extremely busy with her successful career, she always found time for us. Her work in the theatre, film, radio, writing, television programmes, and the inevitable touring, was all-absorbing, yet she took time to write to us from all over the world and somehow managed to attend prize-giving celebrations, chair AGMs and write articles for *The Woman Journalist*.

At the start of these chronicles, Council would like to offer warmest appreciation to their Life President, President and Patrons who support the Society in every possible way.

- Baroness Williams of Crosby has been our Honorary Life President since May 2003. Society members welcomed her following the death of Lady Longford the previous year. Shirley Williams, as she is better known, has a strong family tie with the Society. Her mother, Vera Brittain, was the Vice-President and then Life President until her death in 1970. Baroness Williams entered Parliament in 1964, served in the Cabinet and has held numerous high

SWWJ Life President Shirley Williams, Baroness Williams of Crosby.

Joyce Grenfell with theatrical friends. From left to right: Joyce Grenfell, Val Gielgud, Dame Sybil Thorndike, Rosalind Wade, Robert Harris, Mary Wimbush and Sir Lewis Casson. Country Members' Day, 1966.

political appointments. With an impressive list of honorary doctorates, she has held high academic positions, including Honorary Fellow of Somerville College, Oxford, from where she graduated in 1948.

- Nina Bawden became President in 1980, following in the footsteps of Joyce Grenfell. Nina's writing career spans more than fifty years, during which she produced more than twenty adult novels and seventeen books for children. All writers owe a debt to Nina and her colleagues on the Public Lending Rights team. She mentions the Society in her autobiography *In My Own Time* (Virago Press). This was chosen by P.D. James (*Daily Mail*), Jill Paton Walsh (*The Sunday Express*) and David Holloway The *Daily Telegraph*) as 'Book of the Year' and is a beautifully written account of her life.

- Lady Edna Healey has been our Patron since 1998. She read English at Oxford where she met her future husband, later Lord Denis Healey, moving to Keighley, Yorkshire, and Bromley, Kent, to teach during the Blitz. She has made two documentary films for Scottish Television and is the author of a number of best-selling biographies. Lady Healey has lectured extensively both in Britain and abroad and travelled widely with her husband. She enjoys helping local writers and has supported the Society in every way. She herself began writing at sixty and feels at this time of life people have both the energy and experience to make a serious contribution to contemporary writing.

- Lord Randolph Quirk became a Patron of the Society in 1995 and is a Fellow of University College London. As Professor of English Language and Literature, he is also a Trustee of the Wolfson Foundation. One of Lord Quirk's favourite enterprises was the 'London University Summer School of English' which was immensely successful. He initially became involved with the Society during its Literacy Campaign in 1994 and has since supported every project involving children's education. His loyal support is invaluable.

- Alexander Macmillan, the 2nd Earl of Stockton, became a Patron in our Centenary year in 1994. He inherited his title in 1986 on the death of his grandfather, Harold Macmillan, the former British Prime Minister. Lord Stockton has had a distinguished career in publishing and is President of the Macmillan Publishing Group. He has a long record of helping to further the cause of literacy and has always supported the Society in its educational endeavours. Lord Stockton has always taken a keen interest in the Society and we are delighted to have his valuable support.

- Sir Tim Rice joined us as a Patron in 1995 and is a good friend to the Society. His mother Joan was our much-loved Vice-Chairman during the early 1970s. Sir Tim is an Oscar-winning lyricist known worldwide for his versatile and prolific work. Together with Andrew Lloyd Webber, he broke box office records around the world with three of the greatest musicals of the twentieth century, *Evita*, *Joseph and the Amazing Technicolor Dreamcoat* and *Jesus Christ Superstar*. He first became involved as our Guest of Honour at the ninety-fifth anniversary in 1989 and has since attended many of our celebrations and special Summer Festivals.

Lady Healey and former Chairman Beryl Cross.

SWWJ Patron Sir Tim Rice and Honorary President Nina Bawden.

one

# *Early Days*

## Fleet Street in the 1890s

Although the Society of Women Journalists was created very much with women in mind, the concept was the brainchild of a man – a clever, enterprising newspaperman – Mr Joseph Snell Wood. The year was 1894 and this wealthy, charismatic forty-one-year-old was at the height of his career. Bustling Fleet Street was his domain, lit at dusk by gas lamps, where he dodged 'growlers' and horse-drawn hansom cabs, trying to make himself heard against the incessant thumping from huge newspaper presses deep in the basements of London's national 'dailies' which competed with the clatter of horses' hooves on the cobbles.

Mr Snell Wood knew the newspaper world well. He appears to have had an affable disposition. He was on good terms with everyone, from the cream of aristocracy to the copyboy in his own newspaper office. He had been the Managing Director of *The Gentlewoman,* a best-seller since the early 1890s, and he knew what would interest the upper-class woman. As Director of *The Daily Graphic* and *The Bystander,* employing several females on his staff, he seems to have been a fair-minded employer with good rapport and understanding of the difficulties that the 'New Women' – those females desiring a career in hitherto masculine jobs – were experiencing.

Clubland in the last quarter of Queen Victoria's reign was part of the upper crust's social life. Men's clubs proliferated in the world of newspapers. There were certainly plenty of them around Fleet Street, along with chop houses such as the Cheshire Cheese, made famous a century earlier by Dr Samuel Johnson, restaurants and pubs, such as El Vino's, and small beerhouses nestling around Paternoster Row.

The Society's founder, Mr Joseph Snell Wood.

The *Gentlewoman*, owned by Mr Snell Wood, one of the most popular periodicals from its launch in 1890. This edition dates from the birth of the Society.

Upper-class women also had their clubs. These, though, were mainly of a social, religious or charitable nature. The Primrose League – the women's Conservative organisation – was popular, along with several emerging political groups dedicated to obtaining votes for women. A few years after the Society was founded, Millicent Fawcett, sister of Elizabeth Garrett Anderson (the first woman doctor), formed the National Union of Women's Suffrage Societies. This brought together, under a national umbrella, all the associations that had fought for votes for women.

Women with a predilection for writing presumably already knew of Frances Low's association, formed in 1891, for both sexes, simply called the Writers' Club. This talented woman came from a hard-working journalistic family. Her sister, Florence, was already working as a reporter and their brothers, Maurice and Sidney Low, were both known for their excellence in Fleet Street. Both received a knighthood in 1918 for their services to journalism. Their publication, *Press Work for Women: A Textbook For the Young Woman Journalist* in 1904, was obviously popular with women writers.

Frances had brought together the well-known socialite and journalist Lady Jeune and her friend Princess Helena (third daughter of Queen Victoria). The famous Mrs Arthur Stannard – better known as John Strange Winter – was also an enthusiastic advocate. She hired premises at Hastings House, Norfolk Street, just off the Strand. The club premises then moved to Granville House, Arundel Street, just around the corner.

The beautiful Lady Jeune brought a considerable number of her friends – men and women – to the Writers' Club. These included Thomas Hardy, Madame Sarah Grand, Mrs Humphry Ward, and others who were well-known writers of the time. The Hastings House premises comprised a suite of rooms which included a large drawing room, furnished simply, with an adjacent 'silence' room for writing purposes, a comfortable dressing room and offices. Tea and luncheon were served there, perfect for the 'At Home' rituals that the leisured upper-classes seemed to enjoy at the time.

Although the Writers' Club seems to have been successful as a social organisation, something along more professional lines for woman journalists was needed. This is where Mr Snell Wood came into the story. As a good friend of Lady Jeune, who was making a name for herself contributing to numerous periodicals during the early 1890s, Joseph warmed to the idea of a specialist writing society purely for professional women journalists. At the time they were unrepresented by unions. He felt they should have stronger protection of their rights and aims; assistance in finding work with publishers and agents; and also have the benefit of a solicitor, a private doctor, an oculist and (for some reason) a rhinologist, Dr Octavia Lewin. Eventually, when the positions were established, members enjoyed these free advantages during the following sixty years.

1 May 1894 was the day chosen by Mr Snell Wood to introduce his Society of Women Journalists to the world. There is no doubt that he was regarded as a publishing genius, interested both in the proprietary and in the practical management of the daily and weekly press. Entrepreneurial skills were inherently part of Mr Snell Wood's character – this was obvious even from a young age. Born in 1853, he was an exceptional organiser. Before he was even thirty, he had created 'The Olde English Fayre' and the Shakespearean Show at the Royal Albert Hall. These highly original social adventures created huge public interest at the time, raising more than £10,000 for the Chelsea Hospital in the form of the Chelsea Arts Ball, which was held annually thereafter at the Royal Albert Hall until the 1950s.

Mr Snell Wood also raised £250,000 – a huge amount at the time – for other charitable enterprises, such as Queen Alexandra's appeal for widows and orphans in the Boer War. He was a well-known and respected man in Court circles, being invited in 1901 to become a member of the Organising Committee for raising the Coronation Gift to King Edward VII. He continued his philanthropic work right up until his death in 1920. His granddaughter, Daphne Wood, always a friend of the Society, became a Vice-President in 1984 and attended the Centenary lunch in 1994. She died in January 2009.

## Membership Increases

One of Mr Snell Wood's colleagues was Mr Vavasour Earle, Manager of the London Shoe Company, a friendly man who had generously offered a suite of rooms to the newly-created Society. The address at 116 New Bond Street in London's West End was perfect. Mr Earle arranged for the premises to be redecorated and made ready for the arrival of the ladies. Great excitement greeted the launch, which was mentioned in many of the daily newspapers and in Court Circulars.

During the first few months of the new Society's life in the summer of 1894, 200 women applied to join, paying a subscription of 1 guinea (£60 in modern currency). These members included many from the already established Writers' Club and from the Institute of Journalists which had been founded in 1882 and which boasted sixty-five paid-up female members at this time. A telegraphic address was raised for the Society and appropriately registered as 'SCRIBENDO'. Now the Society was in business! Mr Snell Wood was delighted, and made the following pledge to them:

> I give you my promise to act as your Honorary Organiser in the direction of its affairs, and not leave it till it has become something more than an ordinary success, and I will bear the preliminary expenses until it is regularly constituted and in working order. One of its chief aims is the cultivation of friendly relationship with employers, so that it may become a centre of information to which Editors and Publishers will apply when needing the services of clever and capable women writers and artists.

Victorian woman writers. There were numerous woman freelance writers at the time the Society began in 1894. Some worked for Mr Snell Wood on *The Gentlewoman*.

He was true to his word. For the first three years of the Society's existence, he did just that – endorsing his promise to the letter, paying initial set-up costs, providing advice and generously helping with contacts and introductions. A well-known and influential man in Fleet Street, he opened many doors for members of his fledgling society. The members responded to Mr Snell Wood's generosity by presenting him with a silver punch bowl.

## The First Council

How we would love to see those first meeting minutes and correspondence, but so much of the Society's earliest archives have been lost in fires, floods and during several wars. However, there is much interesting information in the few precious minute books and early copies of *The Bureau Circular*, the forerunner of *The Woman Journalist*, later *The Woman Writer*, magazines.

An unexpected source has come, surprisingly, from the Internet. Much information has been lodged in the form of university Women's Studies courses around the world and these, added to private letters, diary extracts and long-standing members' memories and

("JOHN OLIVER HOBBES.")

*Left* Mrs Pearl Craigie, the American-born novelist whom Mr Snell Wood approached to become the Society's first President. She was succeeded by Mrs Charlotte Eliza Humphry.

*Right* Fanny Strutt-Cavell in 1911, a member of the first SWWJ Council.

anecdotes, have helped considerably in discovering a veritable treasure trove of history. We are able to glimpse just a little of the pioneering spirit of those earlier members. A General Council was appointed during that first year. Many of the leading woman writers of the time were invited to join, the majority being journalists.

From the first official report dated 1895-96, we learn that Mrs Pearl Craigie (1867-1906) better known under her pseudonym, John Oliver Hobbes, was the Society's first President. Mrs Craigie, an American-born writer, had become a household name in the years leading up to the 1890s. Charlotte Eliza Humphry (1851-1925) also joined and there were no less than twenty-five Vice-Presidents, including Marie Louise Belloc Lowndes (sister of Hilaire Belloc). Mrs Jack Johnson, who wrote under the pseudonym of Levana in *The Gentlewoman*, became the Society's first Honorary Secretary.

Among the Vice-Presidents chosen by Mr Snell Wood were Mlle de Bovet, a leading writer at *Figaro*, Mrs Clarke of *The Lady*, Mrs Talbot Coke of *Hearth and Home*, Lady Colin Campbell of *The World,* Mrs Humphry of *Truth Magazine,* Miss Hamm of the *Daily Mail* and *Express* based in New York, Mrs Panton of *The Gentlewoman* and Mrs Elizabeth O'Connor, wife of one of the most powerful men in the late Victorian newspaper world, Thomas Power O'Connor MP, whose bust still dominates the corner of Fleet Street today. Not part of Council, but very much involved with the Society, was Lady Jeune, who had helped establish the Writers' Club and was very much a celebrity as a novelist and much sought-after journalist. At the start of the twentieth century, twenty-six men, many of them distinguished Fleet Street editors, were listed as Honorary Members.

The first Annual Report of Council stated:

Your Council is more than grateful to report that the project set forth, in the Foundation Scheme in February 1894, has been realised even beyond what has been anticipated.

Suffragettes on the march in London, 1908.

Former President Madame Sara Grand (front row, centre) with writing colleagues.

Chairmen and Council members were elected annually during those formative years. Mrs Charlotte Eliza Humphry followed Pearl Craigie. She was well-known as 'Madge' of *Truth Magazine.*

Along with the changing officers of Council, four positions rarely altered. These were the Hon. Physician, the Hon. Oculist, the Hon. Rhinologist and probably the most important, from a writers' professional point of view, the Hon. Solicitor, the last one being Mr Stanley Evans.

Three years after the Society of Women Journalists was formed, Lady Colin Campbell (1853-1911), one of the original Council members, wrote an interesting pamphlet that gives us an indication of the difficulties that female journalists were encountering at the end of the nineteenth century which, even today, seem strangely familiar:

> As it seems that there is a good deal of ignorance and misapprehension existing with regard to the ends and aims of the Society of Women Journalists, I have been asked to set forth briefly the reason why it was called into existence, and the advantages which membership confers upon women journalists. This is above all, an age of combination. Aesop's fable of the bundle of sticks has its wisdom illustrated daily on all sides; but until the year 1894, the large and increasing band of women writers on the daily and weekly press were simply units – often dissentious units I regret to say – to whom the power to be gained by association had never been revealed.

When the original rules of the Society were drawn up in the 1890s, the founder declared that politics and religion were best avoided in the running of the organisation, a difficult stance for the numerous members involved in writing for London newspapers. However, most appear to have adhered to his wishes, leaving political views at home. However, some of the pioneers had links with Parliament – in quite different ways.

During the last years of the nineteenth century, we know that several members were keen on taking up the Women's Suffrage cause, yet incongruously, Council members rarely seemed to discuss national current affairs, let alone allow them to be minuted. Within the few Council minute books that are in the archive, we do know that Mrs Charlotte Despard had asked two members to put her up for election to the Society. The year was 1911 and Council members were aware of Mrs Despard's notoriety from the days of the London Mud March when she had led the 3,000-strong parade of women from Hyde Park Corner in February 1907. She later became leader of the Women's Freedom League. Needless to say, the Society must have allowed her entry as her name appeared in the membership book of 1913, which exists in the archives.

It is strange to read that although the Society President in 1908, Mrs Humphry Ward, was a keen advocate of women's social and municipal work, she was a leader of the Anti-Suffrage movement. As thousands were working for the enfranchisement of women, she sincerely believed this to be wrong. It seems impossible that a woman of her intellect and interests wished to withhold the Parliamentary vote for women. When her year as President was completed, she was succeeded by Mrs J.R. Green (Alice Stopford Green) the wife of the historian, a passionate Irish nationalist. She moved from her London home in Kensington Square in 1918 and lived the rest of her life in Dublin.

# two

# *A New Century*

The Society was approaching its seventh birthday when Queen Victoria died on 22 January 1901. She had ruled her nation for almost sixty-four years, yet it seems strange that the status of women and the quality of elementary children's education were abysmal. Throughout her far-flung empire, women generally had benefited in only a very small measure from having a woman in so prominent a position.

Early in 1901, greetings from Theodore Roosevelt, the President of the United States, were sent to King Edward VII of the United Kingdom, marking the first transatlantic radio transmission originating in the United States. So began Edwardian Britain, a decade which was described by Lord Hattersley as 'a golden sunlit afternoon – personified by its genial and self-indulgent King'. The period between Queen Victoria's death and the outbreak of the First World War appears to have been a remarkable watershed in British history. The Edwardians witnessed huge changes on every level in the world around them.

As the twentieth century opened, in every sphere of life – education, employment, marriage, finance, legal and political rights, inheritance, social status – women knew they had a long way to go before they could be said to be equal to men. The thorny topic of equal pay was uppermost in the minds of professional women – and unfortunately this continues a century later.

Although little is mentioned in the Society meeting minutes, we are able to catch up on world events through private letters, diaries and archival notes. Two national events were mentioned as affecting the social and financial side of the Society, both of which give interesting glimpses into the background of contemporary life and times. One was the sudden cancellation of a party owing to the postponement of Edward VII's Coronation. Another was the mention of the resignation of several members 'who owing to the bad times occasioned by the war', found they were unable to pay their subscriptions. This almost casual note brought the terrible effects of the Boer War closer to home.

Mr Snell Wood, as a leading Fleet Street newspaper editor, was on good terms with many of the leading politicians of the day and it was he who invited some to take an interest in the Society. Several did, and became Honorary Members and Patrons. Often their wives took membership and their names appear in the early journals. This was useful from a publicity viewpoint, as Society events were often mentioned in Westminster and Court Circle

Mr Henry Ford, who introduced his Model T to the world during the early years of the twentieth century. (Photograph by kind permission of Ford Motor Company Archive)

reports. The Cholmondeley Room in the House of Lords was used occasionally for special celebrations and meetings.

Journalists invariably choose to be at the centre of world events as well as everyday life. During the first years of the new century, members reporting for the popular press were writing about the innovations in technology and transport. The American brothers, Orville and Wilbur Wright, were regularly in the news having launched their amazing flying machine in 1903. This absorbed the nation's interest and reams of column inches were devoted to this and to another American, Henry Ford. His brand new motorcar was also receiving huge publicity, as his wondrous new horseless carriage gradually became a common sight on city streets. The introduction of the motor car provided enterprising women journalists with excellent copy for features profiling the paraphernalia, new equipment, clothing and etiquette for this new age.

Mrs Crawford became President in 1902 and Mrs Arthur Stannard became the Chairman. The latter was better known under her pen name, John Strange Winter. Her books had become best-sellers and her name stood foremost among the authors of the time.

## Training

By these early Edwardian times, Britain was brimming with the excitement of innovation and change. From diaries and reports of the time written by female journalists, with the accession of Edward VII to the throne women were beginning to branch out into jobs that traditionally had been the province of men. Typewriting and journalism topped the list of preferred professions for women at that time. This gave members of the Society the idea of training young women. It opened a School of Journalism in rooms it found within Johnson's Court, just off Fleet Street.

The proprietors were several Council members, Mrs Humphry, Mrs Stannard and the Honorary Secretary, Miss Bulstrode. They were joined by Baroness de Bertouch, Madamoiselle de Bovet, then working for *Figaro*, plus a few other high-ranking journalists of the day. Shorthand, typewriting and both literary and commercial correspondence were taught and the school seems to have been successful at the time. This notice appeared in *Home Life Monthly Magazine* in 1903:

> The Society of Women Journalists does a great deal of excellent work in a quiet, unostentatious manner. It is for that reason, perhaps, that its object is not so well known as it deserved to be. It has done much towards improving the position of women journalists, and the advantages of belonging to it are numerous, for it protects both the professional and personal interest of all its members. There is much to be said also for its recreative side, not the least attractive of which is a series of lectures by well-known men, for it throws open its doors on these occasions

to the other sex. The Society members had the pleasure lately, of listening to a man's view of 'Journalism for women' from an able exponent, Mr B Fletcher-Robinson, Editor of *Vanity Fair* who addressed them on this subject. The lecturer gave some valuable hints, which would be of special advantage to beginners, and also related some humorous experiences of his own career. An interesting debate followed, in which some of the most prominent members took part.

## Women's Suffrage

Edwardian England, at least for the middle and upper classes, teemed with the excitement of change and innovation. A new political party, the Independent Labour Party, had emerged. The radical spirit of the early years of the twentieth century was typified by the demand for Home Rule and 'Votes for Women' campaigns and many of the Society's own members were in the vanguard.

On the Society of Women Journalists' Council (as it was then known) there were several London members whose names crop up as the authors of pamphlets and material for the Women's Suffrage movement. As well as women journalists, novelists and poets, the Society attracted practitioners from the Arts and Crafts Movement, to which many females flocked. Several photographers and professional artists joined their ranks.

Although the Society was progressive and encouraged its members to stride into the men's world, it is surprising that Mrs Humphry Ward, the twelfth President, who believed so strongly in the need for higher education for girls – becoming Secretary of Somerville College, Oxford – actively opposed women's right to vote, becoming the first President of the Anti-Suffrage League in 1908.

Exactly a century later, present-day Society member Elizabeth Lord wrote her best-selling book *Give me Tomorrow,* in which she uses the Women's Suffrage movement as a contemporary backdrop.

During that first decade of the twentieth century, women were producing every imaginable type of prose in magazine articles, novels, poems, biographies, travel books, religious commentaries, histories and economic and scientific works. All too often, works by women, and resources about women writers, are hard to find as many either used their husband's name or pseudonyms.

## Remembering 1910

Great changes came in 1910 for the country and for the Society. The nine-year reign of King Edward VII ended with his death in May. Lady McLaren, President that year, received an acknowledgement from

Elizabeth Lord, prolific author and SWWJ member, with her novel set against the Women's Suffrage movement.

Buckingham Palace from Queen Alexandra in reply to the Society's letter of condolence. The country immediately went into deep mourning, as was shown by the front cover of *The Bureau Circular,* forerunner of *The Woman Journalist* magazine.

Two happier events occurred in 1910. On 10 February, Joyce Grenfell (née Phipps) was born. She later became one of our most famous Presidents, playing a vital role in the life and times of the Society. A few months later, on 20 July 1910, Veronica Wedgwood (later to become an honoured Patron) was born. She became one of England's most distinguished historians and was made a Dame of the British Empire. She was a Patron for more than thirty years from the 1960s.

Another important event at this time was the introduction of *The Woman Journalist.* The first edition was issued on 1 December 1910. Also that year, the members moved from 1 Cliffords Inn. Apparently, very little notice was given and there was a feeling of panic as Council members were forced to leave quickly. With the move to new premises in May 1910 to 10 St Bride's Avenue, overlooking St Bride's Church, just up the alleyway from Fleet Street, members relaxed and seemed happy with their new, enlarged, 'modern' premises.

Theodora Roscoe, later a Chairman, who had researched the Society's earliest years, described the move from Clifford's Inn:

> In March 1910, to the dismay of the Council and members, the Society had notice to quit, as a large portion of the Inn was to be demolished to make room for a more modern building. Quarter day was upon them and they were without a home. Happily a friend came to their rescue in the form of Stanley Paul who lent them two rooms in his new publishing office at 31 Essex Street and there they stayed for six weeks. To turn back a year from this flit from Clifford's Inn, it was in 1910 that the Society issued the first number of *The Woman Journalist* which was an expansion of *The Bureau Circular.* By April of the next year the advertisements justified the venture of the little bi-monthly with a cover; all announcements were made through it and it was sent free to every member. As a memento of the Society's former home, now razed to the ground, the frontispiece of the Report bore an engraving of No 1 Clifford's Inn, 'a remnant of old London'.

In 1910, records show that more than twenty influential names appeared on the roster of Society Vice-Presidents. The list of Honorary members included editors from many of the leading Fleet Street newspapers of the time. This was the year when the 'Presidential Badge' was inaugurated, but like most things then, it had to be paid for. Members were invited to subscribe to a special fund raised for the purpose. A note in the journal suggests 'subscriptions which must not exceed one shilling, should be sent to the Hon. Treasurer'. During 1910 an employment bureau for SWJ members specialising in reporting work was established, but was short-lived. Among the list of supporters that year were Lord Northcliffe, Owen Seaman and W.L.O. Courtney. Lectures were given by T.P. O'Connor MP on 'Literary Criticism', Professor Herkomer on 'The Art Life' and William Pett Ridge on 'Dialect & Dialogue'.

A view from the Palace of Westminster towards St Stephen's Tower. The shorthand writers working for Hansard before the First World War were predominantly male.

## Coronation Year

On 22 June 1911 George V was crowned at Westminster Abbey. The events of the day were described and illustrated in *The Sphere*. Due to the agreeable relations at Court, Mrs Bedford Fenwick – President at the time – represented the Society of Women Journalists. There were 300 members and guests present at the Society's Coronation Dinner at the Criterion restaurant on 20 June 1911. The new President presided over a guest list of the cream of London society. Four leading daily newspapers and two clubs were represented at special tables, as well as the Presidents of *The Lady* and *The Woman at Home,* along with the President of The Ladies' Army and Navy Club and Madame Thayer, a good friend of the Society, representing the Lyceum Club. King George and Queen Mary sent thanks to 'the members of the Society of Women Journalists for the loyal message and good wishes contained in your telegram which their Majesties have received with much pleasure.'

Several members living in Wales wrote about the investiture of the Prince of Wales at Caernarfon Castle on 13 July 1911. It had been the first time for 300 years that such an investiture was made, and the first at the castle.

Visits from Parliamentary members to Stationers' Hall or to other venues, including St Bride's Avenue, were frequent and in the November 1915 edition of *The Woman Journalist*, we read of the visit of Sir James Dods Shaw, Editor of the Parliamentary Debates who lectured on the function and duties of the Hansard office:

> I daresay a good many of you ladies have not much knowledge of how verbatim reports of statements in Parliament are managed. It may interest you to know that the reporters in the House of Commons go on duty for ten or fifteen minutes at a time. Lady typists transcribe the notes and they are then sent to the printers and work carries on during the night, no matter how long the debate continues, the [Hansard] Report arrives next morning. It is very quick and accurate work. I have a staff of twelve of the most skilled and accurate shorthand writers to be found anywhere in London. They are not only good shorthand writers, but they are extremely well acquainted with the procedure of Parliament and the personnel of its members. They know the name of every man in the House. They are gentlemen of education and culture, some of them with University degrees.

At the time, the shorthand writers were male. How surprised Sir James would have been to know that in 1979, when some of the Society members visited the Hansard offices, procedure had scarcely changed over the sixty intervening years. Even more interesting is that the Editor of Hansard in 2010 will be a woman.

# three

## *Joyce Grenfell*

The Society of Women Writers & Journalists had been in existence for more than fifty years when Joyce Grenfell became President in 1957. She had already been a member since 1943 and had attended meetings and major events whenever she could.

To the famous Clemence Dane, an earlier President from the 1930s, we owe a debt, for it was she who suggested that Joyce join the Society. The minutes of a meeting, dated 29 November 1943, reported that Joyce had been elected as a Town Member, along with another newcomer, the distinguished author Vera Brittain.

At the time, London was war-torn. The Society members' own special church, St Bride's, just off Fleet Street, had been badly bombed in 1940, as had their favourite venue, Stationers' Hall. This ancient livery hall, belonging to the Worshipful Company of Stationers & Newspaper Makers, had served them well as a regular meeting place for many years, but had also received direct bombardment in 1941. However, it had been patched up sufficiently to allow meetings to take place.

When Joyce agreed to have her name put forward by Winifred Ashton (pseudonym Clemence Dane), she did so on the proviso that due to her busy life as a writer, theatrical performer and BBC broadcaster, she might not always be able to attend regular events. Magically though, she managed to come along to many meetings, particularly the annual Country Members' Day lunches. She contributed articles to *The Woman Journalist* magazine and there were notes and humorous verses passed to her Society friends via Clemence Dane which were read out in her absence at meetings. Within a year, Joyce had been made a Vice-President.

May 1944 was a special time for the Society. Their fiftieth anniversary celebrations took place at Stationers' Hall as planned. It had been hoped that Joyce might have been guest speaker, but at the time she was in Baghdad working for ENSA (Entertainments National Service Association, nicknamed 'Every Night Something Awful' by its members), touring the Middle East and India. Her wartime journals were later published under the title *The Time of My Life: Entertaining the Troops*. Her superb singing and comedic talents on stage led to offers to appear in films. Although she performed in many films, she continued her recording career, producing a number of amusing albums.

But let's look back a century to Joyce's early life. She was born on 10 February 1910, the eldest child and only daughter of an American mother, Nora Langhorne, and architect

Vera Brittain joined the Society in 1943. (Photograph by kind permission of McMaster University Library, Hamilton, Ontario)

Paul Phipps. Her early years sound blissful. She grew up performing at family parties and social gatherings, often with her mother, who was herself a talented musician with a vibrant personality. Joyce adored her younger brother, Tommy.

Joyce's maternal aunt, Nancy, Lady Astor, was the first woman to take her seat in the House of Commons as a Member of Parliament in 1919. She owned a large house, Cliveden in Buckinghamshire. Joyce loved Cliveden, where she and Tommy had spent much of their school holidays, meeting many of the world's eminent politicians and literary figures. Joyce remembered chatting with George Bernard Shaw and Walter De La Mare, frequent visitors to Cliveden.

The Francis Holland School in London was Joyce's first school, followed by the Christian Science School, Clear View, in South Norwood. Joyce went off to Paris in 1927 to attend a 'finishing school'. Wanting to pursue a career in the theatre, Joyce applied and was accepted for a course at the Royal Academy of Dramatic Art, but left after one term. By then, in 1927, she had met Reggie Grenfell and they married two years later at St Margaret's, Westminster. They remained married for almost fifty years until Joyce's death in 1979. Shortly after Joyce's marriage, her parents divorced and Nora moved back to America with her new husband. Joyce missed her mother tremendously and corresponded with her constantly. Despite being born three-quarters American, she was quintessentially English in character. Joyce, in her late twenties, dipped her toe into the world of writing and acting.

From an early age, Joyce had invented characters and pretended to be other people. Being funny and imaginative came easily to her. She was inspired greatly by her mother, Nora, and by a distant cousin of her father, Ruth Draper, who was the original famous American monologue artist. Joyce was good at sketching and enjoyed writing verse. In 1929, She and Reggie were living in a cottage on the Cliveden Estate lent by Aunt Nancy. It was whilst at a luncheon party at Cliveden that she met the Editor of *The Observer* and mentioned her enjoyment of listening to daytime wireless. She was offered the chance of writing the first radio critic column in the paper, a job she loved over the next two years.

In 1936 she sent her first pieces of poetry to the prestigious *Punch* magazine and was published for the first time. Her best friend, the talented writer Virginia Graham, also enjoyed writing verse and was instrumental in sending some of Joyce's work off to *Punch*. The Autumn edition of 1936 shows examples of their poetry.

In Janie Hampton's book *Joyce & Ginnie – The Letters of Joyce Grenfell and Virginia Graham,* we learn so much about the everyday lives of these talented writers. Virginia and Joyce had met at their first school in 1917 when they were seven. They were inseparable friends until Joyce's death sixty-two years later, phoning each other or writing almost daily whenever they were apart.

Magnificent Cliveden, Buckinghamshire. The home of Joyce Grenfell's maternal Aunt Nancy, Lady Astor.

Although Joyce and Reggie never had children of their own, she doted on her friend Verily Anderson's young family. The two met when Verily, an author, broadcaster, journalist and member of the Society, was commissioned to write an article on the star. They became firm friends and Verily's daughter, the author Janie Hampton, always referred to Joyce as a 'fairy godmother' who secretly filled Christmas stockings, left pretty clothes for them, cooked and brought round meals when Verily was ill and even bought a house for the widowed Verily and her five children.

When recalling her introduction to the world of entertainment, Joyce invariably mentioned that special date, 13 January 1939, when she and Reggie had supper with Stephen Potter, a young radio producer. He was so impressed with her impersonation of the speaker she had seen at a local Women's Institute meeting that he offered her a part in *The Little Revue* – the first performance opening in April to full houses and rave reviews. By the summer of 1939, Joyce was commuting from Cliveden to London for the eight performances a week.

War was declared in September that year. On Noel Coward's recommendation, Joyce joined ENSA. ENSA had the task of arranging entertainment for the troops both at home and abroad. Joyce's work with them took her around England and Northern Ireland touring military hospitals, and then overseas, eventually visiting fourteen countries in all, including India, Egypt and several in North Africa. Joyce's time with ENSA was an education for her as a performer, and she later described how the experience helped her to develop her 'working muscles', teaching her how to think on her feet and put on a good show no matter how difficult the circumstances.

When the war ended, Joyce collaborated with Stephen Potter in writing for the BBC's *How* series and, during the 1950s, she became well-known as a supporting actress in films such as *The Happiest Days of your Life* and *Belles of St Trinian's*. She appeared in more than twenty films. However, Joyce Grenfell is best remembered for her one-woman shows and monologues, including the popular character of a harassed nursery schoolteacher who could frequently be heard saying, 'George – don't do that'. Her popularity increased

Although Joyce was busy with her career, she always found time to write to her family and friends. These letters make a superb social history of contemporary times.

when she appeared on the classical music television quiz *Face the Music*. Although best known for her monologues, Joyce was also a talented lyricist, working with such composers as Benjamin Britten and Richard Addinsell.

Joyce was also blessed with wonderful zest, living life to the full and joyfully presenting her remarkable performances in the world of entertainment. She always came across as a cheerful and positive person who had a tremendous sense of purpose and energy. As a devoted Christian Scientist, her religion influenced every aspect of her life and she displayed tremendous kindness and generosity towards others.

Rarely could a performer lay claim to have entertained King George VI and Queen Elizabeth, Laurence Olivier, Igor Stravinsky, Maurice Chevalier and the present Queen during her career. But then, few entertainers possessed the talent, humour and vivacity of Joyce Grenfell.

From the time she met members of the Society, Joyce seemed to feel at home. She enjoyed her role as President, writing in the second part of her autobiography, *In Pleasant Places*:

When Clemence Dane, who was President of the Society, retired, I was elected to take her place. This Society, of which I am fond, is a small one – not just for reasons of exclusiveness but because of the feeling that a membership of not more than six hundred is about right for the kind of intimate and agreeable assembly it is; and also for the services it aims to provide. It is not a hard-bitten or thrusting group caught up in the rat race of journalist-writers, but rather a collection of women who write professionally for many and various markets, including all the media.

As President, my job is to be a figurehead and an observer – benevolent and concerned, in a parental kind of way – but nevertheless a figurehead. So I feel a degree removed, and free to speak in the Society's praise. As I have never been much of a joiner, I can't compare the SWWJ with other societies and associations, but I suspect that there is something unusually refreshing – in an age of fierce party-political allegiances, vested interest, prejudiced and elbowing competitiveness – about a non-political, open-minded group such as this small and friendly collection of writers, whose love for their chosen craft is their reason for coming together. I added to my enjoyable list of 'fringe benefit' the name of the SWWJ.

Clemence Dane at the height of her career in 1920.

From her autobiographies, we learn that Joyce enjoyed the book signing tours. However tiring, she always had a smile and a cheerful comment.

In 1973 Joyce lost the sight in an eye following an infection. It was typical of her no-nonsense nature that she retired quietly from the stage without fuss or fanfare. She continued to work in television, appearing regularly on television's musical quiz show *Face the Music* and contributing to Radio 4's *Thought for the Day*, but the main focus of her creative life became her writing. Over the following six years she wrote two volumes of her autobiography, telling her story from her early life and career right up to her final performance in 1973 – a private occasion for the Queen and her guests at Windsor Castle. In 1976, her autobiography, *Joyce Grenfell Requests the Pleasure*, was published and on Radio 4 in 1977, as part of the *Woman's Hour Serial*, she read it in fifteen parts. Janet Quigley abridged the text and Pat McLoughlin produced the programme which is now in the BBC Radio Collection.

In 1979, Joyce had an operation to remove her blind eye, which had become cancerous, and she died a month later aged sixty-nine. When a Thanksgiving Service was held for Joyce at Westminster Abbey on 7 February 1980, people came from all over the world to remember her and take what places were available in the Abbey. Joyce's lifelong friend, Virginia Graham, once commented that Joyce had an incredibly rare talent for being 'funny without being malicious', and this gift has ensured that her remarkable collection of songs, sketches and writings are as popular now as in her lifetime. In 1988, Maureen Lipman appeared in the hit one-woman show *Re-Joyce*, based around Joyce's songs and sketches, and more recently she has recorded some of Joyce's material under the title *Choice Grenfell*. More than thirty years after her death, interest in Joyce continues.

Older Society members who knew Joyce still miss her. Many have their own special memories of the times they shared with her. Although she was among the best of that rare breed of professional entertainers who could hold an audience on their own, she was also a vibrant, happy person remembered for her laughter, inspiration and joy. She wrote these incomparable words which are a wonderful testimony to a special lady:

> If I should go before the rest of you
> Break not a flower nor inscribe a stone
> Nor when I'm gone speak in a Sunday voice
> But be the usual selves that I have known.
> Weep, if you must,
> Parting is hell,
> But life goes on,
> So sing as well.

# four

# The Woman Writer

## Keeping in Touch

In December 1910, sixteen years after the Society was founded, with the energetic Emily Tait as Chairman and Lady McLaren, the new President, at the helm, Council voted to bring out a four-page magazine, calling it *The Woman Journalist*. This was to continue being published (with a hiatus in 1921-22) for ninety years until the Millennium year, when it was renamed *The Woman Writer*.

Its forerunner, *The Bureau Circular*, a two-page newsletter, had been adequate enough in its time to keep members in touch, but a more substantial journal was required. With five postal deliveries a day in London being normal, there were no complaints about the post.

With so much information and lack of space, the point size was reduced by the printers, making it difficult to read. It had columns boasting of members' published work, items of interest including the introduction of new newspapers and periodicals and the demise of others. There were titbits and gossip about Fleet Street and the newspaper world, the theatre and the arts. As the Society had strong links with the Royal Family, Council's activities were often mentioned in Court Circulars. Titled people were on the membership list and frequently turned up at social events, special receptions and dinners held at prestigious hotels and restaurants.

Subscriptions, due on 1 May for the year 1910-11, were 1 guinea for members living in London and half this amount for country members. This subscription stayed static for many years. *The Bureau Circular* for May 1910 was particularly poignant, as follows:

---

# EDWARD R.I. ⋆

'With profound grief, we record the death of our Sovereign, King Edward the Seventh, at Buckingham Palace on sixth of May, fifteen minutes before midnight, in the sixty-ninth year of his age and the tenth of his reign. King, by the Grace of God, Edward the Seventh worked unceasingly at the most regal task of promoting the welfare and peace of his people, confirming the noblest traditions of the Throne, and strengthening the dignity of his realms, and by his generous humanity attached the love and honour of his subjects to his gracious person as well as to this august office.

We mourn with our beloved Queen Alexandra and all the Royal Family. And to King George the Fifth and his Consort, Queen Mary, we humbly offer our loyal duty.'

---

(⋆*Rex Imperat*) The phraseology typifies the deep respect that subjects expressed for the Royal Family at this time.

## New offices

In 1910 the Society offices were at 10 St Bride's Avenue, a 'home-from-home' for members. It consisted of several rooms in which to work and socialise. Tea parties were popular and members of Council worked on hostess rotas. The office opened daily from ten o'clock to one o'clock and from two o'clock to five o'clock (with the exception of Saturdays). It is interesting a century later to wander down the lane (described earlier as an alley) alongside St Bride's Church. This is where *The Woman Journalist* was worked on by its Editor, then given as Miss Gertrude Burford-Rawlings, but editors changed constantly. When ready for printing, it was delivered by hand to the Women's Printing Society Limited on Brick Street, Piccadilly.

## Matters of Interest

The regular columns were fascinating. Under 'Items Of Interest' we see new publications such as *Laughter Grim and Gay,* the title of a new illustrated satirical paper edited by Mr H. Richardson, formerly lead writer on Messrs Hulton's series of papers; *Clubland,* a new periodical for club-goers; *The Empire Illustrated*, promoting the cause of Tariff Reform, of interest both to those at home and to the Colonists; *The Photographic Monthly* which was to be reduced in price to 2*d* and *Smart Society*, a new magazine published by the Anglo-American Publications firm which was heralded to be a 'winner'.

We read that Lady McLaren was planning a Royal reception on 27 June and that Mrs Alec Tweedie had organised a dinner to which she had invited Sir Hiram Maxim, Lord Shaw of Dunfermline, Lady Jeffson and the Mexican and Chinese Ambassadors, among other luminaries.

In the next edition of *The Bureau Circular*, Council announced they would be sanctioning the insertion of approved advertisements of a character likely to be of interest and service to members, which they hoped would defray the costs of printing. A 'Wants Column' for members to insert miscellaneous notices for a fee of sixpence per three lines was thought to be a daring innovation. There are just a few early editions of *The Woman Journalist* in the archive from before the First World War, but we know that the magazine was published regularly, albeit reduced again to a double-page broadsheet. From a few minute books we learn how members fared during the First World War, savings that had to be made, visits to munitions factories and constant requests for members to contribute financially to war funds.

## Lady Brittain Steps In

At the end of the First World War, the Society was at a low ebb. Membership and finances were down. By 1921 the Society was seriously considering winding itself up. Then Lady Alida Brittain stepped in, joining the Society. She provided financial help, as well as bringing her influence and many writing friends of her husband, Sir Harry, into the Society.

Although *The Woman Journalist* was not published from 1921-22, with the help of Lady Brittain and her newly-formed Council, a new enlarged magazine was launched in January 1923. Queen Mary sent a special message to appear in the first number of the new magazine. Lady Brittain's watchwords in her introductory letter to magazine recipients were 'Patriotism and Progress'. The message received from Buckingham Palace states:

> The Queen learns with much interest that in January 1923 the Society of Women Journalists will issue the first number of their new magazine '*The Woman Journalist*'. Her Majesty understands that the main object of the publication will be to form a link between women writers throughout the Empire. The Queen sincerely hopes that the magazine will have a happy and prosperous career.

The magazine prospered, as did the Society in the following twenty years. Published six times a year, there were many editors, most remaining anonymous, but we discovered that Anne Robertson Coupar, whilst also working on her day job at *The Daily Express*, was Editor during 1944. She produced her first issue of *The Woman Journalist* after being bombed out of her home, sleeping in her Fleet Street office while under almost constant attack. This edition was rather special and welcomed in its bright orange cover – loved by some, hated by others – and described as 'Siberian wallflower', with its distinctive logo designed by the industrious writer/artist Emily Aitken for the Society's fiftieth jubilee anniversary, celebrated in May 1944.

In June 1947, Veronica Mileson became Editor and introduced 'Portraits', the start of a series of members' profiles. Ruth Cobb was featured as her first personality. A regular contributor to the BBC, Ruth was a clever illustrator and playwright, whose work often appeared in *Punch* magazine. Illustrations and photographs in the form of 'blocks' used for newspapers and magazines were then welcomed. This note appeared in March/April 1948:

Blocking all Members

We should be glad to receive blocks of all members – town, country and overseas – suitable for insertion in *The Woman Journalist*. Blocks are costly and ready made ones would reduce expenses. Any block sent in will be returned after use if the owner wishes. We have a set of blocks, which can be re-used, but it means confronting readers with the friendly old familiar faces. Let's have some new pictures. They will help near and distant members to know one another by sight – and it is better to vote for a face than a name on a ballot sheet. The more blocks we have the brighter our columns.

# Recruiting

By May 1949, the magazine had reached eighteen pages. The paper shortage was still in operation and yet the activities, events and book reviews were such that editors wanted more space. Between fifty and eighty writing recruits were then applying annually to join. In the 'Diary Notes' column, we read about weekly discussion groups, regular 'At Home' gatherings and the then popular Brains Trust gatherings at Stationers' Hall. There was a fully stocked library with current magazines. French lessons were also popular.

The third Annual Festival Report in 1949 was published listing the distinguished judges. These included John Masefield, Terence Rattigan, Edward Shanks and Noel Streatfeild among other eminent names. Unfortunately, John Masefield became gravely ill and his place was taken by Margaret Hamerton. Small advertisements brought in a little revenue via Vicky Haynes, listed as Hon. Advertisement Manager in November 1950. Vicky became Editor of *The Woman Journalist* a few years later, followed by Doris Hubbard and Pat Garrod, an amazingly well-connected journalist and playwright.

Theodora Roscoe wrote in January 1951:

I would like to see *The Woman Journalist* in a different format, one that is more the size of *The Spectator* or *John O'London's Weekly*, but not yet… till paper is less precious – perhaps in two years?

# Contributors

With more pages to fill, the Editor began asking members to contribute articles. From the early 1950s, some well-known writers were sending in short features. Vera Brittain wrote a fascinating piece entitled 'On Being a Free-Lance' in March 1951. Helena Normanton was also mentioned in that issue. Vicky Haynes became Editor in spring 1953.

In June 1955, *The Woman Journalist* published an impressive list of speakers who came to Stationers' Hall. Vera Brittain gave an inspiring talk about Olive Schreiner. Ursula Bloom came in July, emphasising the value of cultivating personal contacts with editors, agents and publishers. There was a cocktail party to honour a large group of Canadian women journalists touring Europe and this was fully reported.

In the November 1955 edition, the topic of 'Flats for Women' was mentioned. Phyllis Deakin, then Chairman, was planning to create a scheme to build accommodation for women in the city at Amen Court. Mortgages for single women were then difficult to attain.

Nancy Braham became Editor in 1956, followed by Marie Oxenford and then Vera Burtt in 1957. The irrepressible Pat Garrod took over the editorship in spring 1958. Pat was initially assisted by Jean Finucane, then Marjorie Evans, but in 1961 the hard-working Joan Livermore became Associate Editor and a strong editorial alliance came into being which was to last more than twenty years until Pat's death in 1982.

# Name Change

Many changes followed. In 1951, the title of almost sixty years – the Society of Women Journalists - became the Society of Women Writers & Journalists, but no change was made to the monogram until 1959 when the Society endowed a stall in St Bride's Church. This stall bears the letters in gold, SWWJ, on a blue background in a Gothic design and the title of the Society with its date of origin – 1894 – in white letters on black, polished ebony was specially designed by Roland Collins. As today, Council was always trying to produce interesting events. The Royal Scottish Corporation Hall, Fetter Lane, became the next venue. Lunchtimes and evening meetings with refreshments (made by members) were enjoyed.

By 1959 paper was more readily available. However, an eagle-eye was kept on postage and expenses. Pat Garrod was able to incorporate news in as much as thirty pages, although keeping within the basic postal rate. Her genius in persuading some of the most famous writers of the time to share their experiences with us was remarkable. Rumer Godden, Olive Manning, Alison Uttley, Barbara Pym, J.G. Ballard, J.B. Priestley, Sir Compton Mackenzie and Daphne du Maurier all contributed to the magazine, none of whom ever asked for a fee.

In her summer 1960 journal, Pat reported on a 'symposium' of writers including Rosalind Wade, Barbara Pym, Oliver Moxon and Diana Raymond. Barbara Pym

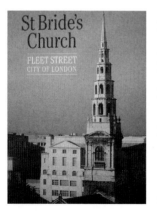

admitted that she put a lot of her own experience, personal thoughts and feelings into her books. In spring 1967, her eminent contributors included Vera Brittain, Laurens Van der Post, Storm Jameson and Penelope Wallace, the latter writing about life with her famous father, Edgar, and the Tallies Press, which he founded, to publish *The Four Just Men*, which had previously been rejected by a dozen publishers.

St Bride's Church, London, 'the cathedral of Fleet Street'.

*Left* Vice-Presidents Jean Bowden, Pauline Graham and Jocelyn Glegg, Editor of *The Woman Journalist* for many years.

*Right* Vice-President and former Editor, Barbara Haynes.

# Farewell to Pat Garrod

Sadly, after twenty-two years in the Editor's chair, Pat died and the Society felt her loss deeply. Members gathered in February 1983 for her memorial service at St Bride's Church, where she had regularly worshipped. Pat's associate of twenty years, Joan Livermore, handed the magazine to the safekeeping of Jocelyn Glegg, who had joined the Society in 1973.

Jocelyn was also Chairman from 1980-82. As an experienced broadcaster, scriptwriter and interviewer, living and working overseas for many years, Jocelyn was a true professional. She had lived in nine countries, broadcasting with radio stations in Sarawak, Borneo, Malaysia and finally Fiji in the South Pacific. Jocelyn brought an exciting and imaginative style to the magazine, introducing bright new covers, clever photography and fascinating features. She knew that *The Woman Journalist* was the Society's showcase and the magazine flourished.

In 1991, Barbara Haynes began assisting Jocelyn with editorial work. Barbara had joined the Society in 1972. Her earlier career embraced her work as a journalist, short story writer and author of numerous books, and she had also broadcast on the BBC. The two made an excellent duo. One new aspect was to record the most interesting features of the current issue onto tape, which Mary Rensten then dispatched to members with eyesight problems.

Barbara was appointed sole Editor in spring 1995. She had held many jobs on Council including Vice-Chairman, Chairman, Welfare Officer and was caring and efficient. Marian Anderson was a super proof-reader who gave Barbara much help when her eyesight problems worsened. Barbara's farewell as Editor was published in the Winter 1999 edition.

*Left*  Valerie Dunmore, SWWJ Chairman from 2004–08. Now Vice-President Envoy.

*Right*  From left to right, Samantha Pearce, Silja Swaby and Penny Legg. On 1 January 2009, Penny took over the editorship of *The Woman Writer*.

## Millennium Changes

Four major changes came in with the Millennium. Spring 2000 brought Doreen Friend as the new Editor. Doreen, a busy journalist who had won awards for her plays, enjoyed her new task. The magazine name changed to *The Woman Writer,* colour was added and the twenty-page issue became larger, now sized A4. Doreen's first feature comprised appreciative features on both Barbara and Jocelyn, who between them had given such unstinting, long service. Both were appointed Vice-Presidents.

Jennie Lisney, who had been the Society's PR Officer for many years, then Chairman in summer 2000, followed in September 2002 as the new Editor. Jennie, too, had been a journalist and publisher of national periodicals and produced an excellent magazine for her members.

June 2004 brought Valerie Dunmore to the Chair and the Editor's torch was handed to Jean Morris, who had understudied Jennie for a while. Jean made an excellent job of the June 2004 issue. Within, she included a poignant obituary dedicated to the memory of Irene Swarbrick, written by Eileen, Lady Ryder. Irene had done so much for the Society, setting up the now flourishing North West Group, and was greatly missed. Jean Morris introduced a smaller sized journal in February 2007 and this was continued by Ann Hamilton, who took over the reins as Editor later that year.

## New Editor

Penny Legg picked up the editorial baton in January 2009. Penny, an experienced freelance journalist and photographer, well travelled, with wide writing experience and interests, is multi-talented with enormous energy. Penny combines all the vital ingredients required for this exacting job. She has introduced new ideas and *The Woman Writer* is vigorous, colourful and, above all, full of inspirational news and views for the good times ahead.

# five

# Overseas Members

## Worldwide Membership

The pioneers hoped that women journalists around the world would join them. They foresaw a 'truly International Society – one that would unite women writers across the seas'. By the end of the twentieth century, they welcomed members who came to London from Europe, India, Africa, America, Canada, and Australia. And to make this known, they stated on the front of their magazines that this brand new association was for:

> Women engaged in journalism either as writers, or as artists in black and white, in the United Kingdom, the Dominions, the Colonies and abroad and for promoting and protecting the personal and professional interest of its members.

With Queen Victoria as Empress of India, there was obviously great interest in that country. Flora Annie Steel was, in the 1890s, a best-selling author of novels set in India. An energetic and well-loved President during the First World War, Mary Frances Billington, the only woman journalist on *The Daily Telegraph*, was invited to cover the Coronation Durbar of George V at Delhi in 1911.

One of the Society's first 'overseas members' was the Maharani of Bhainagar, who was a great friend of the President of the time, Mrs Arthur Henniker. The Maharani had been awarded the coveted Kaiser i Noor for services to India, historically the first Indian woman journalist.

## Letter from America

Just after the turn of the twentieth century, the Society enjoyed a large presence in the USA. Numerous American journalists and authors travelled regularly to London, receiving a warm welcome. They enthusiastically mentioned the Society in American journals. In 1902, Elizabeth L. Banks arrived in London. Even at the age of thirty-two, she had led an exciting life working as a reporter in Wisconsin. Contemporary papers at the time called her an international phenomenon following a series she wrote, aptly titled *Campaigns of Curiosity.*

Following in the footsteps of the pioneering woman journalist Nellie Bly, later to make London her home for a while, Banks gained notoriety through undercover assignments as a stunt girl. She investigated and publicised the working conditions of women in London. Through her articles, Banks demonstrated the capability of women for positions in newsrooms and other traditionally male-dominated places to which women sought entry. Years later, another American journalist, Betty Ross, caused a sensation with her work *Reporter in Petticoats* when it was published in the 1940s.

# Big Game Hunting

Travel writers were attracted to the Society in the early days. One exceptional and intrepid member was Agnes Elsie Thorpe OBE (Agnes Herbert, 1873-1960). Born near Manchester, England, Agnes married at eighteen and moved with her husband William to Vancouver Island, British Columbia. The marriage failed and in 1900, Agnes and baby daughter, Violet, returned to England. The following year she and her cousin, Cecily, embarked on big game hunting. They travelled by passenger ship to Aden, bound for Berbera, Somaliland. Agnes shot game from rhinoceros to warthogs and was mauled and almost killed by a lion, but was saved by Cecily. She travelled widely thereafter to Alaska and Eastern Europe. Agnes' experiences were used within her travel books, the first, *Two Dianas in Somaliland*, was published in 1907.

Agnes became Editor of the *Writers' & Artists' Yearbook*. On 1 January 1931, she received a letter from King George V inviting her to Buckingham Palace to receive the Insignia of the Order of the British Empire for her valued work as a distinguished contributor to writing and as the Editor of the *Writers' and Artists' Year Book* from 1923-29.

Agnes was Society Vice-President in 1939. Her daughter, Violet Bradda Field (1893-1957), also a hard-working member, became a distinguished writer and was awarded the coveted Femina-Vie Heureuse Prize in 1934.

Among many overseas members, Miss M.C. Bruce, was described in *The Woman Journalist* as 'one of our Colonial members' and enjoyed, in 1909, seeing her work regularly published in *The Queen,* one famous feature being 'Union Day in Johannesburg'.

*The Woman Journalist* was published, albeit in flimsy form, throughout the First World War. In the January 1915 edition, we learn from our correspondent in Copenhagen that:

> Although English and French words are now banished from German speech and writings, there is one English word which cannot be got rid of – 'copyright'. Patriots have threatened to boycott publications on which it appears, but as the United States government recognises no substitute, the German publisher who desires to protect his 'copyright' in America, must perforce make use of this word and no other.

In 1924, former President, Miss E. Almaz Stout, an expert on Anglo-Indian life, was signing her latest book *Red Records*, published by Skeffington, price 7s 6d.

Agnes Elsie Thorpe (pseudonym Agnes Herbert) became a Vice-President. Later she was Editor of the *Writers' & Artists' Yearbook* and was awarded the OBE in 1931.

In 1928, we learn much of South Africa's social history from members who worked on regional newspapers. Margaret Whiting Spilhause of Simon's Town was on the editorial staff of the *Cape Argus* and she also freelanced for many of the South African newspapers.

Helen Colt, the Society's energetic Paris representative, was a superb ambassador for the Society between the two world wars. She travelled regularly between Paris and London. She is mentioned in minutes throughout the 1930s. This hard-working newspaperwoman had travelled widely and wrote many books, copies of which were presented to the Society library.

In the September 1946 edition of *The Woman Journalist*, several Council members give accounts of being able to travel freely to former occupied countries. Violette Bilham wrote from Trieste:

I left London on July 11, had a break in Paris, lunch in Lyon, tea in Marseilles, dinner in Pisa. Next day I flew to Naples, then on to Rome, dining at the Brufani Palace in Perugia. Next day I drove through Florence and Bologna going straight to Trieste. I've just joined my husband and am working in the Features Department of the Allied Information Service. Whew!

In October 1938, one of our overseas members, Gwen Rogers, wrote her autobiography, telling the story of an English woman's sixty adventurous years between 1876 and 1936 in South Africa. Entitled *I-Alone*, this book became a best-seller and was reviewed across the South African press.

# The Games

The London Olympics of 1948 brought thousands of overseas visitors, especially from America. Council members gathered in London to entertain some of the British Olympic team and journalists covering the events. Miss Kruger, the sports correspondent of the German News Agency DPD, who had been in England as a Prisoner of War, had returned

Dr Tessa Nelson-Humphries, long-standing member living in New Mexico.

under happier auspices to report for her newspaper.

In the November 1948 issue of *The Woman Journalist*, we read reports from Lusaka, then capital of Northern Rhodesia, and from New York, British Columbia. The New Zealand Women's Writers & Artists Society, founded in 1932, kept in constant touch. Several members reported from Malaya. Members of the Society of Women Writers of New South Wales were keen to send in their news and enjoyed seeing this published in *The Woman Journalist*.

During Jean Winder's trip to America in March 1955, she described how Mrs Eleanor Roosevelt had recently decided to hold press conferences attended by women journalists only, thus forcing the appointment of more females to newspaper staffs. Often sixty women reporters were present at regular Monday gatherings which the First Lady used for correcting any misapprehension about her public speeches.

Dr Tessa Nelson-Humphries has been a member of the Society since 1970, first in Kentucky, USA, where she was Professor of English, then in New Mexico in 1990. Tessa has won numerous Society awards for her wonderful articles and poetry and her letters are full of wit and fun. She was awarded the coveted 'Woman of Achievement 1984' by the Business & Professional Women's Club of Williamsburg for her writing expertise and services to education. We appreciate Tessa's continuing presence and contribution to the Society.

Betty Fry in New Zealand is another successful, talented writer and her articles and poetry anthologies are a joy to read. We learn much about her fascinating life in England and New Zealand in the interesting reports she has sent to *The Woman Writer* over the years. We have enjoyed reading news from many other members in Tasmania and Australia.

Pamela Payne joined the Society in 1977 and was the only overseas member in Belgium, where her husband served with NATO in Brussels. Pamela's journalistic career began on *The Marlow Times* and *Farnham Castle* newspapers. She continued her freelance writing career in the various countries in which she lived, running weekend writing seminars for the British Council in Naples where she founded a multi-national Writers' Circle. She taught creative writing at the Petersfield Adult Education College and is proud of the fact that many of her students, at home and abroad, are now published. Her own book, *Voices of Petersfield and District,* is selling well. Pamela served nine happy years on the Council as the Speakers' Secretary.

During Joyce Grenfell's book-signing tour of Australia in 1978, she paid a flying visit to see her friends Nancy and Vincent Fairfax. They all went off into the bush to meet up with some of the members of the Society's sister writing group in New South Wales. Joyce was thrilled to be asked to formally open the bull sale that was taking place that day. Ever-enthusiastic, she amused everyone present at the Eidsvold Station Santa Gertrudis Bull Sale with her rendition of 'Happy Bull-Sale to You.'

Cynthia Wong (who used two pseudonyms, Yu Huen and Tsing Hwa) was born in Malaysia of Chinese parents. She was Principal of Pui Chung College in Hong King, as well as being one of the founders of Eton English Schools and Chairman of the Hong Kong Anglo-Chinese Schools Association. Cynthia visited us in London on several Country Members' Day events.

From the 1980s, there was a steady recruitment of members from all parts of Africa, Australia, Israel, Canada, Sweden and Germany, joining with many members from America, Canada and the Arab States.

Elizabeth Wallace, from Denver, Colorado, brings us regular news from the glorious mountains of this part of America. A journalist, broadcaster and author of five books, Elizabeth founded the Castle Rock Writers' Circle in 1999. She is a member of the distinguished Denver Woman's Press Club, which is proud of its 110 year provenance. Elizabeth sends news about her writing successes and manages to visit England several times a year on book-signing tours.

Judy Pollard Smith joined the SWWJ in 1994 and is an active member in Hamilton, Ontario. Judy has won several prizes for her short stories and her work is regularly published internationally. Also living in Hamilton is Betty Saunders, another excellent writer who keeps us up to date with her current projects.

Jacqueline Cooper, the talented and prolific writer living in Switzerland, is also an active member of the Geneva Writers Association. Jackie's latest books for children are seeing record sales. She visits the group whenever the Summer Festivals take place in London.

Noreen Riols, a British-born member living near Versailles, is a prolific writer. Noreen's experiences during the Second World War are fascinating and she has written about them in her book *Katharine – Love and Drama in War-torn Britain*, the first of a four-book saga, *The Ardnakil Chronicles*. She was attached to Special Operations Executive, working alongside the celebrated Colonel Maurice Buckmaster. Noreen's personal involvement with SOE remained a secret until the official files were opened in the Millennium year. Then television and press descended. Noreen appeared on television in the BBC 2 four-part documentary film *Secret Agent*, which summarises her experiences while working at Beaulieu in F Section. Noreen is now the sole survivor of just six women who worked at HQ. It is always wonderful to meet Noreen at SWWJ luncheons and this year she attended the Summer Festival.

Humour is not an easy genre, but Maggie Van Ostrand in California manages to attract huge audiences to her websites, linking her readers across the world. Much of her work is published online, as well as in hard copy. She can teach us much about self-syndication. She writes brilliant keynote convention speeches and has interviewed the best of American celebrity.

In 2005, Society members gave a festive welcome to the editorial staff of the *Women of China* magazine. As usual, the Christmas lunch was held at the New Cavendish Club. The delegation from China was organised by the State Bureau of Foreign Expert Affairs of the People's Republic of China. Since then, several members have contributed features to the *Woman of China* magazine which is that country's most successful periodical.

One of the latest overseas members is Daniela Norris, who is truly international. Born in Romania, she grew up in Israel and Canada and has lived and worked in Jerusalem,

Joan Moules, prolific author from Sussex, and Noreen Riols, overseas member living in France.

Toronto, Nairobi, Luanda and Paris and now lives in a small village not far from Geneva, Switzerland. She attended the 2007 Swanwick Writers' Summer School where she met member Jean Currie, who sang the SWWJ's praises, and is pleased to be part of the Society.

The distinguished author and journalist, Muneeza Shamsie living in Karachi, has been one of our most prolific writers. A loyal member for twenty years, she keeps us up to date with news from Pakistan. She has contributed features, interviews and book reviews to newspapers and journals worldwide. Whenever possible, Muneeza tries to synchronise her business meetings with visits to meet fellow members at the New Cavendish Club.

Members living abroad seem to appreciate the link with their special Overseas Liaison Officer who tries to offer help and guidance. Over the last fifty years, these Council members have included Phyllis Deakin, Edith MacWhirter, Eileen Huckbody, Daphne Moss, Gwynneth Ashby, Sylvia Kent and Phyllis Ellis-Franks, who took office in 2008.

# six

# *Country Forum*

## Out and About

From the 1960s onwards, literary visits became popular. Under the leadership of Victoria Kingsley, Edith Bacon and Susan Muir, members filled coaches destined for Dorset and Thomas Hardy country, to Chichester to see a matinee, Cromer in north Norfolk to visit long-standing member Verily Anderson's home at Northrepps, and to Shrewsbury where members stayed at the stately Prince Rupert Hotel (single room 15s) where they could explore Stokesay and Ludlow Castles. There were rambles around Epping Forest in Essex arranged by Joyce Elsden, followed by an excellent lunch. Every summer, invitations arrived from the Chairman of the time to visit her at home. Theodora Roscoe, Julia Cairns and Clemence Dane loved entertaining members, particularly Clemence who, although living in a flat in London's Covent Garden, owned a trio of caravans in Midhurst, Sussex.

## Country Members' Day/Summer Festival

Town members obviously enjoyed meeting their colleagues in their trips around England, which led to the idea of Country Members' Day in May 1962. Alex Colbrook, then Treasurer, instituted the present form of Country Members' Day, which was a combination of AGM, prize-giving and a chance to meet members living outside the London area.

The first Country Members' Day was held on 15 May 1962 at the Royal Scottish Corporation Hall in Fetter

Julia Cairns (Mrs Paul Davidson), Council member and Poetry Advisor. A wonderful prose writer and poet. A trophy is dedicated to her for Poetry Competitions.

Lane. Jean Bowden and Verily Anderson were both there to welcome guests. The AGM was held and Rosalind Wade took over from retiring Chairman, Monica Ewer. It is interesting that the cost of membership had only risen from 1 guinea in 1894 to £1 17s 6d for town members and from 10s 6d to £1 1s 6d for Country. President Joyce Grenfell sat alongside Theodora Roscoe and Sir Harry and Lady Brittain. They welcomed members from all around the world. This happy day set the pattern for future AGM/CMDs and some of the most distinguished speakers were invited as guests.

Joyce Grenfell, as President, was able to be present at the Country Members' Day on 25 May 1977 and gave an entertaining talk. Memorably, this was the Queen's Silver Jubilee year and Joan Clifford, in her third year as Chairman, mentioned the approaching celebrations in her report.

# Regional Meetings

From the Society's start in 1894, meetings were held in London. Membership fee was set at 1 guinea for town members and 10s 6d for those living more than twenty miles from the capital. These 'country members' formed a large part of the overall membership.

From the 1912 address book, it is noticeable that the majority of members who lived in the capital were wealthier, often with second homes in the country, but most of the members who worked as journalists on daily newspapers, lived in London. It was relatively easy to keep in close touch with their contemporaries on a regular basis. The journey to London in the early days of the Society was more of a problem for members living in the

The North West Regional meeting in Cheshire, 2006.

Essex Group members with talented writer and film scriptwriter, Jurgen Woolf, guest speaker on their special Annual Writers' Day in Brentwood, Essex, 2008.

country, although many made the effort to attend the Annual General Meetings – the most important gathering on the Society's calendar.

While *The Woman Journalist* magazine kept members around Britain in touch with events throughout the year, it was obvious that most of the activities did take place in London in the years before the Second World War. Council encouraged members to form 'country liaison' or regional groups.

During the 1950s, Bronwen Vizard in Creigian and Joan Leese in Herefordshire invited Society members in their areas to their homes for lunch and to hear a guest speaker. The idea spread and soon others adopted it too, with meetings in Suffolk and Norfolk, which delighted Joan Livermore, who was the brains behind many of the group formations. Joan lived near Jean Gumbrell, whose East Anglian Group was most successful.

When Irene Swarbrick moved from London to Cheshire in 1985, she created the North West Group at Knutsford. Warmth and friendship were on offer in abundance and it certainly worked. Twenty-five years later, the group is still going strong. Since Irene's death in 2004, Frances Hancock has taken over the reins and continues to arrange lunches in and around Cheshire. Many of the Society's northern members such as Chriss McCallum, Maria Atkinson, Peggy Poole, Alison Chisholm, Ann Latham and Muriel Berry have attended from the start and it is good to see that the work of the members of the Society is represented in this part of England.

Jo Clay in Dorset began the Sherborne Group and in 1996 Gwynneth Ashby, as well as being the Overseas Liaison Officer, with a lifetime of travelling around the world collecting material and photographs for her numerous books for schools, invited members to her Christchurch home. This group has expanded and with the help of Philippa Lawrence, this is a special annual event. This group now covers the Dorset, Wiltshire and and Hampshire area and is growing.

The South West regional branch began eight years ago with Southern Group member Jackie Addison-Brown opening her home to members with a wonderful lunch and guest speaker.

Joan Moules and Pauline Hill living in Chichester, Sussex, founded the Southern Region arm of the Society. They began in 2005 and arrange spring and autumn meetings. Morning sessions usually range from discussions on a set topic to workshops. The afternoon sessions are devoted to guest speakers and have included the distinguished author Kate Mosse. Their meetings are well-attended, great fun and give opportunities for networking over a large area,

The first Essex Group met at the Brentwood home of Pat Pound. There have been other venues including the Essex Record Office in Chelmsford, followed by lunch. Brentwood is a useful centre for Essex writers and Brenda Frith hosted an excellent 2009 lunch. Gatherings in Cambridge have taken place, as well as several in Kent. Vice-President Jennie Lisney is the efficient organiser for Regional Meetings and is happy to help members start up local gatherings, particularly in remote areas.

## Continental Trips

Joyce Elsden has always been the brains behind the carefully-planned trips to France, the first of which was to Bayeux during the 1990s. These have taken place every other year since and each one has been excellent, the latest visit being to Paris in 2009. Pat Alderman remembers:

SWWJ trip to Deauville, France, 2007. Joyce Elsden is on the far right.

One of the nice features of Joyce's trips to France is that there are invariably one or two poetry occasions incorporated in them. The year we went to Cormeille in Normandy. We had a hilarious joint evening with the Poetry Society of Cormeille where the guest was Pierre Blondel, renowned French poet and winner of the Prix Gustave Flaubert. They read their poems in French – which Pauline and Fay made an excellent job of translating – and we read ours in English (our visit written up in local press). We also had a wonderful poetry evening in Champagne two years ago where we presented our own and favourite poetry (Pauline and Jean McConnell did some impromptu translations of eighteenth and nineteenth century verse). Some wonderful memories.

# Weekend Schools

The Society's Weekend Schools came into existence quite by chance from a throwaway remark from a Society member who had just returned from a less-than-satisfactory residential weekend in 1966, organised by a well-known commercial writing school.

'We could do better than that for a quarter of the price,' commented *The Woman Journalist* Editor, Pat Garrod. Council member Jean Bowden agreed. The Chairman that year was Elizabeth Harvey. At the next Council meeting, plans for a residential weekend were drawn up for the following year. Celia Cross's organising skills had much to do with the success of this first Weekend School, held on 4-6 April 1967. The venue was 19 Portland Place, the Glass Manufacturing Federation's centre just up the road from the BBC. Member Midge Rider's husband was Chairman of the Federation. The venue proved satisfactory and delegates were accommodated at the University of London's Nutford House in Brown Street, not far away. Celia arranged the catering and this first Weekend School was a runaway success. The cost of £4 10s covered two nights stay, including meals.

The programme over the three days was varied and included a coach tour of 'London by night' for an extra cost of 5s. Jean Bowden, then Assistant Fiction Editor on the *Woman's Own,* arranged an impressive line-up of speakers. This included writing celebrities Ursula Bloom, Mary Howard, Russell Braddon, Susan Muir, Marie Joseph, with radio stars Jack Singleton and Anne Howells (offering tuition on radio writing). With Celia Cross and Jean Bowden's considerable powers of organisation, this first Weekend School set the pattern for the following years.

By the late 1960s the Weekend Schools, held at Nutford House, were programmed for alternate years. They attracted regular numbers of around 130 members who looked forward to a programme that included some of the most famous speakers of the day. Practically every aspect of writing was covered. Council members who played a large part in the Weekend Schools at the time were Helen MacGregor, Edith Bacon and Gerry Lyons. In 1977, the Weekend School was held at King's College, Cambridge. Chairman that year was Joan Clifford and an excellent line-up of speakers and programme of events was enjoyed.

In the intervening years, these events have seen a name change. They are now Weekend Conferences. They follow the pattern of earlier years, featuring talks, discussions and special seminars on a variety of topics of interest to writers. Since the Millennium,

The 2008 Weekend Conference was held in historic Chester.

they have been held in some of England's largest universities, including London Royal Holloway, Cambridge and Chester, all of which were enjoyed by delegates and speakers alike. Cambridge University is the destination, of course, for the 2010 Joyce Grenfell's Weekend Conference, at which Jean Morris and her team hope to meet as many Society members as can attend.

# seven

# *Associations*

## Then and Always

Networking is a word we hear so much about in the business of writing. In times past this was known as 'introductions', so it is nothing new. Mr Snell Wood certainly advocated meeting and making friends with people in Fleet Street. He realised the advantages from his earliest days as a young newspaperman, and later as one of the top newspaper editors in Fleet Street. He encouraged the members of his newly-formed Society to seek fellowship with similarly-minded people. He himself was a member of several city gentlemen's clubs.

Mention has already been made of the Writers' Club started in 1891 by Frances Low, herself a prolific writer, based then at Hastings House, Norfolk Street, just off the Strand. Among its membership were many embryo Suffragists and later members of the Society of Woman Journalists. Whether there was rivalry between the two organisations, we know not, but certainly many of the Writers' Club members swapped their allegiance and paid the 1 guinea fee to join the Society of Woman Journalists. They flocked to their first club quarters at 116 Bond Street, courtesy of Mr Vavasour Earle, a friend of Mr Snell Wood. From Society minutes, we learn they kept up the Hastings House premises on and off for many years.

A contemporary newspaper of the time reported:

> The Woman Journalists' Club is another comparatively new organisation. Its president is Mrs Craigie (John Oliver Hobbes) and it provides a course of lectures during the winter and gives what is known as a midsummer party to which all literary artistic and social London is bidden. In June 1896, this great function was held at Stafford House – the town residence of the Duke and Duchess of Sutherland and there was such a demand for invitations that the committee was forced to announce through the columns of the morning newspaper that no more cards would be issued, those which had been sent having been inexorably marked 'strictly non-transferable'.

The popularity of women's clubs in London at the end of nineteenth century was considerable.

P.D. James (Lady James of Holland Park).

At the top end of the scale were those which aped the exclusivity of the gentlemen's club – the Alexandra (founded in 1884) was restricted to 'ladies of position'; members of the University Club for Ladies (1887) were united by their university education; the temperance Pioneer Club (1892), founded by Mrs Montgomery Massingberd, catered for women with an interest in women's social, political and educational advancement; and those joining the aristocratic Empress Club (1897) could enjoy the benefits of a smoking room and a tickertape for stock market news.

## Society of Authors

Another close connection to the SWWJ has been the Society of Authors, almost from the start of the Society in 1894. The SoA is a non-profit making organisation founded in 1884 by the distinguished writer Walter Besant (1836-1901) and its aim 'to protect the rights and further the interests of authors' remains its objective today.

The SoA's first President was Alfred Lord Tennyson. Some of the greatest names in literature were members and closely involved in the Society's development. Members included George Bernard Shaw, John Galsworthy, Thomas Hardy, H.G. Wells, J.M. Barrie, John Masefield, E.M. Forster and A.P. Herbert, and countless contemporary writers were at the forefront of its activities and campaigns. Dame Veronica Wedgwood, Society Patron for over thirty years, has been a former SoA President. Their current President and Chairman are P.D. James and Margaret Drabble, and Mark Le Fanu is their General Secretary and his staff – who have experience in every aspect of the writing profession – run the day-to-day office. Their present membership stands at around 8,500 and is growing.

## The British Federation of Business & Professional Women

The affiliation to the BFBPW began in 1947 with encouragement from member Phyllis Deakin (1899-1997) who was the founding Honorary Secretary of the British Federation of Business & Professional Women's Clubs of Great Britain. In May 1956, Phyllis, accompanied by Edith MacWhirter, Marie Oxenford, Elizabeth Harvey and Nancy Braham, attended the Eighth Annual Luncheon of the British Federation of Business & Professional Women held at the Connaught Rooms in Holborn. Phyllis was also founder of the Wandsworth Business & Professional Women's Club.

# London Writer Circle

Foyle's Bookshop in Charing Cross Road was the perfect venue for the start of the London Writer Circle, which was founded in 1924. Its pioneers enjoyed fellowship with the Society. Their numbers grew and during the 1970s and '80s they boasted London's most distinguished authors, journalists and poets. Lady Elizabeth Longford was their President, followed, upon her death, by her daughter, Lady Rachel Billington, the acclaimed novelist.

Fellow writers met to offer friendly advice and constructive criticism. Even when London was being bombed in the Second World War, the members met in each others' homes. Their aim was to keep the spirit of the Circle alive. In 1945, LWC re-formed with a new committee, headed by Robert Hunter. Members began flooding to meetings, then held at the Royal Scottish Corporation Hall in Fetter Lane, and then at Caxton Hall, Westminster. LWC can take credit for being the inspiration for the creation of numerous groups, such as the Swanwick Summer School, Brentwood Writers' Circle and Phoenix Poets – all still flourishing. Unfortunately, hiring London venues was difficult and although their newsletter 'Within the Circle' was regularly issued and kept members in touch, meeting rooms changed often following the Millennium. The nucleus of the London Writer Circle now meet at the Royal Festival Hall monthly and welcome all writers.

# Chartered Institute of Journalists

The CIoJ was also founded in 1884, but changed its name to the Institute when it was granted a Royal Charter in 1890 by Queen Victoria. A century later, in 1990, Queen Elizabeth presented the Institute with a Supplemental Charter, enabling it to change its name to the Chartered Institute of Journalists. Membership is open to all bona fide journalists, whether working in newspapers, broadcasting, magazines, press and PR, or as freelancers. The CIoJ seeks to uphold and improve professional standards and represents members in the workplace and, where necessary, in the courts. SWWJ member Susan Elkin was Chairman of the Freelance Division from 2001 until 2005.

# The International Lyceum Club

'A proud past and a promising future' is the keynote message of the distinguished International Lyceum Club. The Society members valued the friendship of Constance Armfield (née Smedley, 1876-1941) who founded the first Lyceum Club in London in 1903. Constance's book *Crusaders* outlines the creation of this important organisation

TO MEET THE SOCIETY OF WOMEN JOURNALISTS.

**MRS. LEONARD REES,**
(Mary MacLeod Moore)

AT HOME

Tuesday, December 9th, *1924* from 4 — 6 p.m.
at the

LYCEUM CLUB, 138, PICCADILLY, W.1.

The Rt. Hon. T. P. O'CONNOR, P.C., M.P.
WILL SPEAK.

Mr. ALFRED NOYES WILL READ FROM HIS OWN POEMS.

R.S.V.P. to Mrs. Leonard Rees, c/o
SOCIETY OF WOMEN JOURNALISTS,
Sentinel House,
48, Southampton Row, W.C.2.

*Left* Invitation to an 'At Home' usually meant much socialising for the upper-classes during the interwar years. The Society enjoyed a strong friendship with the Lyceum Club, which had been founded by one of their own members, Constance Armfield (née Smedley), in 1903.

*Right* Dr Mark Bryant, past Secretary of the London Press Club, with the author Jilly Cooper, who presented the Lynda Lee-Potter trophy in 2005.

which continues to grow around the world. Constance mentioned many pioneering women writers who achieved literary success at the start of the twentieth century.

The Lyceum Club membership grew rapidly alongside that of the Society of Women Journalists and joined the fraternity during luncheons, special anniversaries and festivals. The first International Lyceum Club Congress was held in London in 1912. An early member was Theodora Roscoe, who often stayed at the Lyceum residential clubs in Adelaide and Melbourne. In 1924, the Society Chairman Mrs Leonard Rees (Mary MacLeod Moore) arranged a special 'At Home' at the Lyceum Club in Piccadilly at which the Rt Hon. T. P. O'Connor MP was guest speaker. Alfred Noyes, the distinguished poet, read from his own work.

The Lyceum Clubs celebrated their 100th anniversary in 2004 at the International Congress in Switzerland. Members of numerous Chapters established in major cities around the world met in Basel.

# The Women's Press Club

The irrepressible former chairman Phyllis Deakin was the driving force and first Chairman of the Women's Press Club from its creation in 1943. At the time she was the only woman journalist on *The Times*. The club grew out of Phyllis's annoyance with the then official male-only Press Club's refusal to admit women on to its membership list. Phyllis called a meeting of female journalists in April 1943 at the Falstaff Pub in Fleet Street. There, the sixty-two attendees formed the new group with the aim of allowing women access to a professional network, such as the original Press Club represented, and offering a reception area for visitors to London. Its headquarters were then located at 52 Carey Street and its initial Annual General Meeting was held on 31 October 1944, presided over by Lady Margaret Rhondda, with Phyllis Davies as Vice-Chair and Hilda Grosvenor as Secretary.

Former American First Lady Mrs Eleanor Roosevelt pops into the Women's Press Club in Tooley Street to meet some of her friends, 1959. SWWJ member Elizabeth Hart is top the stairs. (Photograph by kind permission of Anne Bolt's family)

From its heyday in the 1940s, a regular newsletter was issued for members, edited by Anne Temple. Later members included Anne Lansdell, Penelope Wallace, Marjorie Proops, Julia Cairns, Mary Stott and Eileen Elias. Eminent photographers such as Anne Bolt and Janet March-Penney captured the luminaries of the day. Often, the top women editors called in to have lunch and on 12 November 1958, Queen Elizabeth, the Queen Mother, arrived at the Carey Street premises. Margaret Lane (Countess of Huntingdon), then President of the Women's Press Club, showed the Queen Mother around their newly-decorated premises. The following year, Eleanor Roosevelt, America's former First Lady enjoyed the company of the women journalists while paying an impromptu visit to London.

## The London Press Club

Once women were officially allowed to join the London Press Club, many transferred their allegiance following the demise of Phyllis Deakin's Women's Press Club in 1972. The original London Press Club has a prestigious provenance, having been founded in 1882 by George Augustus Sala, a prominent journalist at the time. Familiar visitors from LPC to the SWWJ luncheons, celebrations and the occasional Weekend Conference, have been Dr Mark Bryant, former Secretary of LPC, and Peter Durrant, Company Secretary, both of whom have delivered excellent talks. Members of the two societies have met at Wig & Pen in its heyday, the Cheshire Cheese and El Vino's in Fleet Street, and still look forward to the famous annual Press Ball.

# Swanwick Writers' Summer School

The Swanwick Writers' Summer School in Swanwick, Derbyshire, was established in the summer of 1949. In those heady days, the cost of the whole five-day Summer School was 25s, which included the motor coach journey from London's Victoria Coach Station to Derbyshire. Swanwick's aim is simple – to give advice and encouragement to young writers, as well as to those more experienced in the art of writing. Their first Chairman was Robert W. Hunter, Vice-Chairman of the London Writer Circle and husband of the Society's own secretary, Lynne Hunter. Many SWWJ members have taken part or have tutored courses.

Vice-President Jean Marian Stevens remembers attending Swanwick in the summer of 1950. Jean kept a diary note of that eventful week. We learn of her arrival at The Hayes and being taken on a tour around the lake and gardens, later meeting the fellow delegates and the incomparable Cecil Hunt. During a fascinating week, Jean met and mingled with some of the best in the world of prose, poetry and journalism.

August 2008 marked the sixtieth anniversary of the Writers' Summer School. The organising team celebrated in fine style and the occasion brought hundreds of writers together from around the world. Marion Hough is now its hard-working Chairman.

# The New Cavendish Club

Society members enjoy meeting at the New Cavendish Club at 44 Great Cumberland Place, a stone's throw from Marble Arch. This elegant building, with its roof garden and excellent banqueting services, hosted many Society celebrations over the years. Its own history is fascinating, entwined as it is with the SWWJ in several ways. Since 1959 it has been the London address of the Voluntary Aid Detachment and a portrait of its founder, Lady Ampthill, smiles down at visitors in the reception area.

The VAD was founded in 1909. Its members provided indispensable nursing services in military hospitals, driving ambulances, running canteens and undertaking general nursing war duties.

Former Life President Vera Brittain, herself a VAD nurse, describes in her book *Testament of Youth* her training and life during this terrible war. Princess Mary, the Princess Royal (Countess of Harewood) was a member, along with notable writers, such as Agatha Christie, Naomi Mitchison and Lady Cynthia Asquith. Among the members, there were many who trained and worked with the VAD, including Helen Long, who wrote of their experiences during wartime.

During the summer of 1914 there were over 2,500 Voluntary Aid Detachments in Britain. Their vital work did not stop at the cessation of the First World War. The training and travelling to many parts of the world continued through the ensuing years and their invaluable work was recognised up to the Second World War and after.

Nina Bawden, our President and author of numerous books and plays. She is also a member of PEN.

# PEN

This simple acronym represents poets, playwrights, essayists, editors and novelists and many Society members, such as Marie Belloc Lowndes, Violet Bradda Field and Dame Rebecca West among others, were associated from the start with this international society. Mrs Dawson Scott (1865-1934) founded PEN in 1921.

During its early years, PEN opened centres only in Europe, but writers of other nations joined and by 1926, members from fifteen nations met in Berlin. Today PEN is composed of 141 centres in ninety-nine countries. Its membership is open to all published writers, regardless of nationality, language, race, colour or religion. Each centre acts as an autonomous cultural and intellectual organisation within its own country, and individual centres organise regional conferences and seminars. All centres maintain links with each other through the organisation's headquarters, International PEN.

Its initial purpose was to enable writers to meet and exchange ideas. However, over the years it has increasingly concerned itself with human rights, battling against censorship and giving moral practical support to writers persecuted or imprisoned for their views. Many of the most famous writers were members of PEN, including John Galsworthy, its first President, who was followed by H.G. Wells and later E.M. Forster, Robert Frost, Arthur Miller, W.B. Yeats, James Joyce and Frances King among the world's literary luminaries.

PEN membership includes many the SWWJ's writers since the Second World War, including our globetrotting Betty Ross, who represented the Society in the Stockholm Congress in 1946, and Flora Annie Steel, Marie Stopes, Rosalind Wade, Monica Ewer and, in more modern times, Lady Antonia Fraser, P.D. James, Nina Bawden, Jean Bowden and Pamela Birley. When Joyce Grenfell visited Vancouver in 1958, she met members of the local Women's PEN Club and likened the friendship and entertainment in her honour, to 'that of my own dear Society of Woman Writers & Journalists' back in London.

# Romantic Novelists' Association

This association has a special bond with the Society. Introduced in January 1960, mainly through the efforts of Alex Stuart, it was hugely successful from the start. Denise Robins agreed to be President with Netta Muskett as Vice-President. Barbara Cartland, too, was one of the first Vice-Presidents. In her inaugural speech, she paid tribute to Alex Stuart for starting 'this wonderful crusade' and claimed that romantic novelists were popular because they had 'an enthusiasm for life.' From its original membership of 115, this notable organisation has now expanded to more than 700 members. Many Society members are linked to the RNA, which promotes commercial women's fiction, alongside historical and romantic fiction. Their aim is to encourage good writing in all its variations, to learn more about the craft, and help readers enjoy it.

A scheme for appraisal of manuscripts began and has been a very important element in helping unpublished writers to achieve first time publication. Many of those writers have gone on to become best-selling novelists. The popular novelist, the late Joan Hessayon, was the SWWJ's Vice-Chairman during 1993 and her name lives on in the RNA's annual Joan Hessayon Prize for New Romantic Writers.

# The Authors' Licensing & Collecting Society

The Society has a strong fellowship with the ALCS, a non-profit making organisation run by writers for writers. Maureen Duffy is currently Honorary President. It was formed to secure fair compensation for secondary rights on behalf of writers which provides a vital and necessary income to a diverse selection of people within the creative industries. Any type of writer is eligible to join ALCS. Its eclectic selection of members includes scriptwriters, novelists, poets, academic writers and journalists. Since its inception in 1977, it has distributed over £140 million to writers for their work that has been copied, broadcast or recorded. As the largest writers' organisation in the UK, with a current membership of over 55,000, ALCS is committed to fostering an awareness of intellectual property issues among the writing community and both protecting and promoting authors' rights. It was involved in the setting up of Public Lending Rights, PLR, obtaining funding for writers' not only in the UK, but also across Europe and America. PLR is now celebrating thirty years of helping writers. Many Society members enjoy the financial benefits of membership of ALCS. Also, the SWWJ Council meets regularly and runs workshops at the Writers House, offices of ALCS.

# All Party Parliamentary Writers' Group

The All Party Parliamentary Writers' Group was formed at the behest of ALCS and launched at their AGM in 2007, since which time there have been regular meetings of mutual interest. It is a cross-party group from both Houses of Parliament of around thirty members, founded to protect and promote authors' rights. Its aim is to 'represent the interests of all writers, to

The late Joan Hessayon, a previous Vice-Chairman. The Romantic Novelists' Association have a sponsored competition for new young writers in her memory.

Chawton House, Sandy Lerner's brainchild, housing the Study Centre for English Women's Writing 1620-1830.

safeguard their intellectual property rights and ensure they receive a fair level of recognition and reward for their contribution to the economy and society as a whole'.

Since its inception, it has researched the marketplace of the technological age, especially the World Wide Web. It has challenged the government's intended cuts to PLR. It keeps a watching brief on all legislation in the UK and Europe to ensure fair compensation for creative work. Its website is www.allpartywritersgroup.co.uk.

# Chawton House

Over the last few years Chawton House, once the home of Jane Austen's brother, Edward Austen Knight, has become special to the Society members. Sandy Lerner, co-founder of Cisco Systems in the USA, purchased Chawton House in 2003, fulfilling a dream. It is now a Study Centre for English women's writing from 1620-1830. The Society members are grateful to Sandy and her Council for allowing the Society to display their magnificent silver trophies, the most appropriate place for all to see.

# eight

# *Broadcasting*

## Marconi Makes his Debut

Even as the Society pioneers were designing the layout of the Constitution, a young Italian scientist, Guglielmo Marconi, was working on his project to introduce wireless technology to the world. The year was 1894 – the founding year – and the twenty-year-old, frustrated at not being able to lodge his patent in Italy, left his home in Bologna and arrived in London the following year.

The rest is world history and has been well-documented. Marconi's pioneering work with wireless telegraphy systems resulted in his reputation as the 'Father of Radio'. Marconi built his factory at Chelmsford, Essex, not more than twenty-five miles from Savoy Hill, the address of the first London radio station established in 1922. Within ten years, Broadcasting House was erected on the corner of Portland Place.

## Writing for the BBC

The impact that the introduction of the wireless had on Society members was great. Many were eager to pitch their written work to this magical medium. By the 1930s, the wireless was an accepted part of everyday life. This article in the April-May 1935 edition of *The Woman Journalist* appeared at the time of King George V's Silver Jubilee:

> If the war made the King's reign momentous, science has made it the most amazing on record. Travel by air connects the most distant parts of the Empire. Distance has been annihilated. By Wireless on Jubilee Day, the King at Buckingham Palace will speak to untold millions of his subjects in every quarter of the globe and will, himself, receive their messages of loyal affection. Ere long it may be anticipated Television will reveal the King as a living, speaking presence at firesides throughout the Empire.

*Left* Mr Guglielmo Marconi's statue stands in Chelmsford, Essex.

*Right* The mighty British Broadcasting Corporation building in Portland Street, London.

The Royal Jubilee was indeed celebrated by members with a special luncheon and duly reported in the press. Society members during this time between the two world wars welcomed the chance to earn their living writing for radio.

# Broadcasting Women

One of the pioneer women presenters at the BBC, Elise Sprott (1885-1961) came to work at the London headquarters in 1926. She championed broadcasting for women, becoming the publicity envoy for the BBC, travelling and lecturing on the medium. Earlier she had worked from 1919-23 with the famed Hoover Child Feeding Mission and was then Vice-Convenor of the International Council of Women's Broadcasting and Television Committee. Elise Sprott was one of the first women members on the BBC staff working from Savoy Hill until 1932, when the BBC moved to the purpose-built Broadcasting House in Portland Place. This impressive art deco building quickly became a London landmark and was described as 'a new Tower of London'.

Elise came to the SWWJ via Emily Moore, who made contact when arranging an Empire broadcast to overseas members. Elise was an indefatigable member, who ultimately served as Chairman for many years during and after the Second World War.

Although working prodigiously from her office, she also became the BBC's publicity envoy, travelling worldwide. In 1938, she was awarded the MBE for her services to broadcasting. In the Autumn 1942 edition of *The Woman Journalist*, the Editor reported a special 'Broadcasting Afternoon' for members. They met at 20 Lower Regent Street and were taken behind the scenes by Miss Sprott to experience the work then undertaken by the Overseas Propaganda Departments of the BBC. Her talk was accompanied by records allowing the audience to hear some of the messages sent to the occupied countries.

## Woman's Hour

By 1946, numerous members were giving talks on the *Kitchen Front* and the newly-created *Woman's Hour* which began that year. Mary Manton began giving a series of weekly commentaries to America and in the Summer 1947 edition of *The Woman Journalist*, members Mary Ball, Ann Landell and Margaret Seal were commissioned to give talks on various programmes, including appearances on *In Town Tonight*, with presenters John Ellison and Roy Rich interviewing other members the following year.

Work for freelance journalists and magazine writers had become scarce during the early 1950s due to the desperate paper shortages. However, broadcasting and television compensated and the way was open for writers to pitch their ideas to the BBC.

## Listen with Mother

By January 1952, long-standing Society member, Marie Oxenford, was broadcasting regularly on the Home and Light services. She suggested that members should send scripts to the producer of *Listen With Mother* and considered writing for radio and television to be very well paid. She reported:

> For stories and talks the fee is £1 per minute and stories to be adapted as a play by a member of the BBC staff will be paid 15 shillings per minute for the first twenty minutes and twelve shillings after that. For poems the fee is one and a half guineas for the first 16 lines and 3 guineas from 17 to 24 lines.

Marie suggested in *The Woman Journalist:*

> Try submitting a script to one of the *Children's Hour* programmes. The soundest advice is, listen, to the one of your choice, regularly, over a period of time, till you have got the 'feel' of it. Stories must be short, not more than 750 words and since very young children are realists, they enjoy stories about familiar things, their toys, the trains they watch when they go for walks, the bus at the end of the road.

Consequently, at least a dozen members were submitting work to the BBC – and being paid immediately. During the 1950s, many BBC writers and producers were invited to speak at Society events, including Miss Jonquil Antony who wrote the popular *Mrs Dale's Diary.*

In 1953, Brian Beggs from the BBC came to talk about the Queen's Coronation and his work with the Corporation. Daphne Oxenford, daughter of Marie, had her stories accepted for *Listen with Mother,* as did Verily Anderson, whose play *Leave it to Mother* received acclaim. Daphne became an actress and worked often with Joyce Grenfell on the radio and in the theatre.

## Speakers

Huw Weldon (later Sir Huw) came to talk about television on 8 October 1954. At the time he was BBC Publicity Officer. He explained about the difficulties of production, accentuated by the fact that up to date there was only one wavelength. There was also friction between the studio and the outside broadcasts. Apparently studio productions took three weeks to build up, while the outside programme was built up by events which were televised on the spot, involving a huge amount of work. At this early stage of television, he reckoned that success awaited the writer of a really good three-act farce. 'Television in colour will come, but not yet, the BBC insists that when the time comes, all must have it and not only London.'

The BBC broadcaster and writer Barbara Wace was top of the bill on 15 April 1958 when she gave her audience a lecture on how to write for the BBC, a field then often bypassed by print journalists. Verily Anderson, Society member and regular contributor to the BBC, passed on advice from colleagues. Ruth Drew and the then Editor of *Woman's Hour,* Joanna Scott-Moncrieff, were both regular visitors and encouraged members to keep sending them synopses.

## Pilkington Committee

In 1960, Joyce Grenfell, then Society President, was invited to serve on the Pilkington Committee 'to consider the future of the broadcasting services in the United Kingdom'. She describes the following years of the work on the Committee in her book *Joyce Grenfell – In Pleasant Places.* We learn here about Joyce's debut on radio programmes and the background to television's popular musical quiz *Face the Music,* chaired by the incomparable Joseph Cooper.

## The *Today* Programme

During the twenty-two years that hard-working Pat Garrod was editing *The Woman Journalist,* she persuaded many of the best BBC presenters to either contribute features to the journal or pay a visit to tell members about their programmes and life at the Beeb. Jack de Manio, journalist, broadcaster and presenter of the *Today* programme, was a favourite

Jocelyn Hay,
President of Voice of
the Listener & Viewer,
with colleague
Robert Seatter, 2009.

and they were delighted to read Pat's amusing interview with him in the September 1969 journal. Pat's first impression of Jack was 'of a cheerful, friendly man who made me feel immediately at ease… Jack was awarded the Variety Club of Great Britain's 'Radio Personality of the year'. Jack de Manio's book *To Auntie With Love* is now a collector's item.

## Voice of the Listener and Viewer

Jocelyn Hay joined the Society of Women Writers & Journalists in the early 1970s and was elected to Council in 1987. She organised several memorable London-based Weekend Schools. A successful freelance writer and broadcaster (having started as a volunteer presenter on Forces Radio), her specialities included cookery and crafts on *Woman's Hour*, and the history of Fair Isle and its knitting.

In 1983, she founded Voice of the Listener & Viewer (VLV) and became its Honorary President in 2008. VLV represents the citizen and consumer interests in broadcasting, and speaks for listeners and viewers on all broadcasting issues. She ceased broadcasting in her own right after founding VLV but continued to direct the training agency, London Media Workshops, which specialised in writing and directing radio, television and video programmes until 1994.

Appointed MBE in 1999 and CBE in 2005 for her work with VLV, she was awarded the 'Elizabeth R Award for an Exceptional Contribution to Public Service Broadcasting' by the Commonwealth Broadcasting Association in the same year. In 2007, she was named 'European Woman of the Year (Humanitarian Section)' by the European Women's Association (British Section).

# nine

# *Diversity*

For fifty-seven years, the organisation was known as the Society of Woman Journalists until it added 'Writers' to its title in 1951. It's true that when Mr Snell Wood created the Society in 1894, he was himself a journalist and editor of several newspapers. Many of the earliest members, too, were connected with the world of Fleet Street. It is interesting to learn that when women writers pitched their manuscripts to editors and publishers during the late Victorian period, they often felt forced to abandon both Christian name and surname, using their husband's name or adopted male pseudonyms. For example, the first President, Mrs Pearl Craigie (1867-1906) adopted the pseudonym John Oliver Hobbes. People were astonished to discover this popular best-selling novelist was a woman.

Another successful author was Joseph Shearing, whose real identity, a closely guarded secret for many years, was our member Marjorie Bowen (1886-1952) who used at least ten pen names. In 1941, the writer Phil Strong said, 'She is the best serious writer of high romance now publishing.'

## Changing Names

In keeping with the world changes, the Society kept pace and following the Second World War, the Council of the day felt a change of title was important to reflect the wide variety of members' work. Always democratic, Council sought members' opinion about the change of name and within the November/December 1951 edition of *The Woman Journalist*, this note appeared:

> Arising out of the discussion at the annual General Meeting with regard to adding the word 'Writers' to our title, members will note that, at the September meeting of the Council, it was carried by a large majority that this should be added.
>
> Henceforth, our Society will be known as The Society of Woman Writers & Journalists (SWWJ). It is felt that this wider title covers more accurately the activities of our members. The addition of 'Writers' will be added to the later numbers on the cover of our Journal.

Only a small change, perhaps, but members seemed satisfied with their new name. The world of women's writing had shifted over that half-century, perhaps for their benefit, although that longed-for dream – parity with men's salaries – remains unfulfilled.

## Genres

During the 1940s a large contingent of Society members also belonged to the Women's Press Club started by the famous journalist Phyllis Deakin, a small woman with a huge energy and ability, proud to have been the first woman staff reporter to be appointed to *The Times*. From the early days of our Society, there were many women working in the newspaper world, although rarely were they found sitting in the Editor's chair. Some, however, managed to get to the top, such as Julia Cairns, who was appointed Editor-in-Chief of Weldon Publications between the wars and Alice Head, Director of Country Life. Penelope Wallace, daughter of the distinguished crime writer, Edgar, was Vice-President of the Women's Press Club during the 1950s.

## Variety

By the 1950s, some were, or had been, foreign correspondents and our affiliation to the Women's Press Club brought us into contact with the great names of the time. Members wrote features and books on many diverse topics. Crime writers, playwrights, editors of well-known magazines and regional titles; many more were successful novelists, poets, historians and some of the earliest members wrote on medical matters. Finance, music, art, travel, religion and wine expertise were also on the list of members' CVs.

Throughout the Society's existence, history and biography have been popular genres. Foremost among them were the works of Life President, the late Lady Elizabeth Longford, whose biographies of Royalty and nobility established her among the highest echelon of historical writers. Members treasure their personally signed copies of *Queen Victoria,* one of Lady Longford's most erudite biographies.

Dr C.V. Wedgwood, our Patron and a distinguished historian, was the author of *The Thirty Years War, Oliver Cornwall* and *William the Silent,* which won the James Tait Black Memorial Prize in 1944. Marjorie Bowen and the late Eileen Elias were also well-known for their skilful memoirs and, of course, Joan Moules' biography of Gracie Fields – among other well-known personalities – has been the subject of several radio and television appearances.

A member during the 1920s was Dr Marie Stopes (1880-1958), the British birth control campaigner. She was the first woman to join the Science Faculty of Manchester University in 1904. Her books *Married Love* and *Wise Parenthood,* both published in 1918, caused a sensation around the world. They sold in their millions and were translated into many languages. Her other books on birth control practice sold the moment they were on the bookshelves and are still to be found today. Following the Second World War, she campaigned for birth control in the Far East. She often wrote for *The Woman Journalist* and we have some interesting articles written when she at last became a joyful grandmother.

Ann Ladbury, television star in the 1970s and '80s and a former Chairman.

Listed in the membership files were Ivy Compton-Burnett, Rose Macaulay, Phyllis Bentley, Dame Rebecca West, Ursula Bloom, Richmal Crompton, Angela Thirkell, Berta Ruck, Marie Joseph, Joan Hessayon, Jean Plaidy, Stella Gibbons, Patience Strong, Catherine Cookson and Elizabeth Bowen, among many others. The Chairman from the 1920s, and later President, was Dame Alida Brittain. She was a talented harpist and gifted musician, who wrote articles for numerous newspapers and magazines, and her ballads and compositions are still played today. Many members over the century wrote about musicians, orchestral life and the wider musical world.

Another President of the Society just before the Second World War was Eleanour Sophy Sinclair Rohde (1881-1959), an erudite garden historian and horticultural writer. She collected unusual herb and vegetable varieties, and also worked as a garden designer. One of her best known designs was the herb garden for Lullingstone Castle in Kent. Her books on herb growing are collectors' items.

Food and wine were topics for both our writers and guest speakers. Elizabeth Craig was co-founder of the British Good Housekeeping Institute. Nell Heaton was producing numerous family cookbooks in 1940s and '50s. Myrtle Foster and Lily Douglas were all linked to the Society and Molly Graham, winner of the Bronze Medal of the Gastronomische Akadamie Deutschlands, paid us a visit. Fanny Cradock and her husband, Johnnie, were well received when they spoke at Stationers' Hall in 1976. Pamela Vandyke Price, the expert on wine, was also a popular guest speaker.

Contrast that with the world of Mary Thomas' sewing and knitting books. Mary was the Society's Honorary Literary Adviser throughout the Second World War and her books are collectors' items. Another expert of fashion and dressmaking is member Ann Ladbury, who joined the Society in 1971. Ann became Society Chairman in 1986. With her wonderful personality, appearance and skill with a needle, she was a 'natural' for television and was promptly offered her own television programme devoted to her dressmaking craft. Over an eighteen-year period, Ann travelled, lectured, wrote twenty books, appeared in five BBC series, two ITV series and appeared in her own afternoon television magazine *Houseparty* programme for Southern Television. In April 1953, the Queen's couturier Hardy Amies was a popular guest speaker at Stationers' Hall.

Margery Allingham's success as a crime writer was well-established when she joined us in the mid-1960s and her husband, Philip Youngman, the portrait artist, often came along to Stationers' Hall to talk to members about his work.

Past Chairman, Vice-Chairman and now Vice-President, Jean Bowden has seen more than 100 books published specialising in crime and enjoys a huge readership. Elizabeth

Member Sally Ann Voak and Peter Snow at the SWWJ Summer Festival 2009.

Lord has written twenty-one sagas in as many years. Eve Phillips and Beryl Williams' novels both enjoy continuous readership.

The diversity of members' writing has widened over the years. Pauline Graham, with her clever business acumen, writes about the world of commerce, as does Carol Baker, the Editor of the *Credit Control Journal* and other business periodicals, which have been the basis for several successful books. Diana Wimbs is our copy-writing expert.

Travel and caravanning were the main topics that made Christine Fagg's name well-known in the tourist industry. She remembers joining the Society in 1954, which started off a lifetime of friendship with so many of her Society contemporaries. Christine enjoyed her hectic life as a journalist and became a columnist for numerous caravan journals. She was honoured by having a caravan model named after her. Other SWWJ travel writers include Maria Atkinson and Solange Hando.

The incomparable Joan Clifford, a former Chairman, writes on matters of religion, as does Patricia Batstone, who has assiduously edited church magazines and writes hymns and sermons.

'A history lover' is how Daphne Ayles describes herself. She has been writing for more than seventy years, producing articles, stories and plays, the last of which was commissioned for her local church and later published. She edited the *Rechabites Magazine* for years. Her latest book *On a Clear Day You Can See God*, published by the Emissary Press, has been reprinted.

Vice-President Valerie Dunmore and her colleague and earlier SWWJ member Janet Macdonald wrote for the equestrian market and between them founded the Side-Saddle Association in the mid-1970s. This led to publication in 1978 of their non-fiction book *Riding Side Saddle*. Other members, including Gillian Thornton, write for the equestrian market.

Following in the footsteps of a much earlier member, Marie Corelli, who was famous for her New Age studies and interest in alternative medicine, Council member Josephine Chia writes on similar esoteric themes, as do Joyce Elsden and Judy Hall.

Society members have contributed to and edited some of the popular trade journals, such as Carol Cannavan who edits *Plumbing and Heating Engineering* and *Connected*. Janice Grande also contributes features to these titles. Wendy Hughes has contributed to a wide variety of historical, trade and consumer periodicals. Sylvia Robins is a regular contributor to *The Daily Telegraph* and *Weekend Telegraph* celebrity columns. Sylvie Nickels was a seventeen-year-old Society probationer who excelled from the first time she came to the

Society in the late 1940s. Her short stories and features were published nationally and she became a respected contributor to *The Financial Times, The Daily Telegraph* and travel magazines. She has also written several books in recent years.

An earlier Council member, and now a Dame, Jacqueline Wilson has been tremendously successful writing for the teenage market, as has Susan Skinner, also well-known as a distinguished poet. Lady Eileen Ryder has written numerous children's books and articles on children's education, and Frances Clamp writes for children as well as being a successful local history writer.

Current member Sally Ann Voak has written more than twenty-eight books on nutrition and Eve Bonham Cozens has specialised in sailing and yachting. There is a lively group contributing to writing magazines – Doris Corti and Alison Chisholm on poetry, Vivien Hampshire on novels, Margaret Graham on writing techniques and Chriss McCallum on 'How to…' subjects, to name a few. Jennifer Worth's best-selling non-fiction book *Call the Midwife* is shortly to be made into a film. Today, Society members write on every imaginable subject, including the widening 'chick-lit' genre. An entire library could be created from our members' output.

## Supporting the Cause of Literacy – 1994

For as long as the Society of Women Writers & Journalists has been in existence, the state of children's literacy has been of great importance to members. From archives, we see that over many years – certainly before the present news media headlines over the poor state of children's literacy – members were concerned about this perpetually vexing problem. Despite the billions spent on education, many youngsters are still leaving school hardly able to read and write.

In the sixties, Joyce Grenfell was a patron of the 1963 Campaign for Education, and it was through her that members had the privilege of meeting many distinguished educators and people involved with education. The award-winning screen writer, Robert Bolt, took great interest in the various projects planned by the Society and during his visit in 1963, said he was pleased to have the opportunity of talking to Society members on what he saw as the most vital subject of education, stating that modern society's negative attitude could prove a national disaster for the future state of education.

As one of the special events marking the SWWJ 1994 Centenary year, two distinguished SWWJ members, Dr Joyce Morris, and Christabel Burniston MB, were invited to submit written suggestions for a Literacy Campaign. Dr Morris wrote in the Spring 1993 edition:

> We readily accepted the invitation because we believe that the SWWJ should have a voice in the ongoing debate about literacy standards and how to improve them. After all, professional writers need proficient, enthusiastic readers like themselves, and who is better equipped to focus attention on the essential ingredients of effective writing of various kinds?

Following their carefully monitored survey asking members for their thoughts and opinions on this important controversial subject, the Literacy Seminar took place on 10

Christabel Burniston's ninetieth birthday at the House of Lords. Back row, from left to right: Lord Quirk, Shelagh Snell, Jean McConnell, Susan Elkin, Mary Rensten, Dr Joyce Morris. Front row: Christabel Burnisten and Lady Longford.

March 1994. It was a successful event, attracting widespread press coverage. The panel of seven distinguished speakers included the Rt Hon. John Patten, Secretary of State for Education, eminent novelist Baroness P.D. James, the well-known English scholar Professor Lord Randolph Quirk, Elizabeth Henderson, whose publications include the video 'Early Recognition of Dyslexia', and Jennifer Chew, an expert on the teaching of reading.

A report published in December 1994 entitled 'Professional Writers Support the Cause of Literacy' was prefaced by our then Honorary Life President, Lady Elizabeth Longford. It was a comprehensive compilation of views from 200 members resident in England and fifteen more living in other countries.

Dr Morris summed up this vital project, reporting:

Bearing in mind that the SWWJ had no political affiliation as stressed in the Preface by Lady Longford, the Society Honorary Life President, the Survey findings lend considerable support to the Government's initiatives with regard to family literacy and to the requirements of the National English Curriculum. These, as summarily described by Mr Patten in his contribution to the Seminar Proceedings, do not appear to have been radically changed by Mrs Shephard, the current Secretary of State for Education.

According to 'official' documentation I have recently received, she is strongly in favour of what Christabel Burniston calls the 'oral passport' of Standard English grammar and vocabulary. There is also reason to believe that she would welcome Lord Quirk's *Standard English must be Standard Practice* for its authoritative content on that troublesome subject. Likewise, it is reasonable to suppose that she would approve of what Jennifer Chew has to say about *Spelling* and Elizabeth Henderson about *Teaching Children to Read in the First School*. As for Baroness James' contribution on *Literacy and the Professional Writer*, doubtless it will be appreciated not only by the Education Secretary but by all professional writers who, it is hoped, will follow her suggestions about what they can do to encourage literacy.

Although this project was carried out sixteen years ago, its findings and conclusions are still relevant today.

## Symposium 2008

Dr Morris' enthusiasm for and knowledge of good English were again highlighted at the 2008 Summer Festival held at the Royal Institution of Great Britain on 5 June. During the evening, the Dr Joyce Morris Symposium took place and members listened to a panel of eminent English language professionals give a lecture entitled 'Good English Matters'.

The panel consisted of Barbara Large, Founder Director of Winchester Writers' Conference; Dr Bernard Lamb, Reader in Genetics at Imperial College London; and Dr Christopher Mulvey, Emeritus Professor of English at Winchester and Director of The English Project, which is due to be launched in 2012. Society member Susan Elkin summed up and thanked the contributors.

## Christabel Burniston (1909-2006)

Christabel has been the inspiration for many women writers. In 1953, oral communication was not regarded as a necessary life skill. The fact that spoken English now has a recognised place in the school curriculum is due to a small group of pioneers in the early 1950s, among whom Christabel Burniston was foremost. She founded the English Speaking Board (ESB) in 1953 to give practical recognition to her education vision: that true development of personality, and security in social relationships could only grow through confidence in speaking, listening and acquiring simple oral skills. A gifted examiner, she had a genius for drawing out the best in even the most shy and nervous children, making them feel important and respected as unique individuals. By her own efforts, she took the spirit and philosophy of ESB to New Zealand, Australia, South Africa, Malta and Canada.

# ten

# SWWJ Competitions

## Background

From the earliest times, the Society has recognised the interest and stimulation that competitions bring to members' lives and Council include them as part of the programme each year. In *The Woman Journalist* dated February 1911, a series of open writing competitions were advertised with large cash prizes. They were organised by the then popular *Pearson's Weekly* journal, and many other magazines and newspapers followed this pattern and began organising similar writing projects.

This gave the Society ideas for organising their own open writing contest. From Council minutes of a meeting held in the closing year of the First World War, we note the suggestion put forward to mount a national writing competition, for men and women. An entry fee of 5s was proposed and 1 April 1918 was planned as the launch date. Miss Evelyn Miller volunteered to handle the entries. More than 700 entries were received. Unfortunately, one entry was considered to be so obscene that the police were called and the miscreant – a schoolmaster – was arrested. When the entries were whittled down to the shortlist of fifty and the choice was made, the winner was found to be a member of Council, although she had entered before being co-opted. Nevertheless, she nobly stepped aside to allow a runner-up to receive the award.

Writing competitions have served several purposes in promoting, publicising and encouraging recruitment to the Society. Over the years, Council has used this device on major anniversaries and historical events.

## Adjudication Panels

As well as invitations to enter competitions, members were often called upon to sit on judging panels. In 1920, the Society took over the work of the Femina-Vie Heureuse Prize English Committee. These two French newspapers, *Femina* and *La Vie Heureuse* offered an annual prize of £40 for the best English novel published within a given period. Judges included Viscountess Northcliffe, the then President, Mrs Alice Perrin and Mrs Mary Binstead.

In March 1932, member Violet Bradda Field, the distinguished traveller, and author and daughter of Council member Agnes Herbert OBE, won the coveted Femina- Vie Heureuse prize for her critically acclaimed book *Small Town*.

## The First Literary Festival

The Literary Festival was a forerunner of the Society's Country Members' Day. It developed from an idea put forward by Anne Robertson Coupar, the *Daily Express* journalist, during an informal gathering in Clemence Dane's flat in Covent Garden towards the end of the Second World War.

At the time, the cheerful, hard-working Emily Moore (1884-1978) had just relinquished the role of Treasurer of the Society and immediately became the Hon. Financial Supervisor of the Festival. By her clever management, a cheque from the profits was handed to the Royal Literary Fund for the first four years of the Festival, which was held annually until 1957 – all outstandingly successful.

The first of the Open Literary Festivals over the next decade took place in 1947, although planning had started years earlier. Patrons, Presidents, Vice-Presidents and other friends were asked to present a trophy for the annual competitions. To eliminate futile

1949 Literary Festival scene with Dame Irene Vanbrugh presenting awards.

entries, a nominal charge of *2s 6d* entry fee was to be made and entire proceeds from this source were to be donated to a charitable fund connected with Fleet Street.

To wide publicity, the first Literary Festival took place in 1947. This was an open competition and invitations to enter were publicised at home and abroad.

The six classes were:

- Short story up to 5,000 words
- Feature of 1,000 words suitable for daily press
- 600 word leader on Empire or international topic
- Children's story suitable for broadcasting or magazine, up to 1,000 words
- One-act play for stage, radio or television
- Poem – free verse or traditional form not exceeding twenty-eight lines

Entry fees were donated to the Newspaper Press Fund. The prize-giving was a glittering affair held at Stationers' Hall on 12 June 1947. More than 250 members and guests from national daily newspapers, periodicals, publishers and agents took their places. Members travelled from all over England and there were many visitors from overseas.

## Celebrated Judges

The people approached to judge this first Literary Festival competition were notable celebrities of the writing world: Val Gielgud agreed to judge the one-act play, Cecil Day Lewis received the poetry entries and Ivor Brown and Sidney Gordon judged the press articles. During those years, many of London's leading magazine editors were on Council, such as Brenda Spender, Literary Editor of *Country Life*; Lucie Walker Leigh, London correspondent of Editorial Bell of Argentina; Nancy Braham, who was a regular contributor to *Listen with Mother* on the BBC; Marjorie Evans, a proficient lecturer and freelance writer; Pat Garrod, a successful playwright; and Beryl Irving, an illustrator and writer for Oxford University Press, Blackies and other leading publishers.

## Trophies

Although we have many other trophies, the following are mostly awarded for regular competitions held over the last few years:

- The Lady Violet Astor Rosebowl was dedicated by Lady Astor and is usually awarded for the best-published magazine or newspaper article. Traditionally, it is presented at Country Members' Day. Lady Violet was wife of John Jacob, Lord Astor of Hever, one of the most eminent Patrons during the 1940s and '50s. Lady Violet took a great interest in the Society and presented the award in 1947. Her sons became newspaper proprietors, heading many of the nation's newspapers between the two world wars. Lady Violet died in January 1965 and is buried at Hever Castle.

First prize winner of the Christmas Competition 2008 was Elizabeth Pozzy. Prize-giving and the annual party were held at the New Cavendish Club. From left to right: Dorothy Pope, Elizabeth Pozzy, Chris High (judge) Jean Bowden and Robert Grieve.

- The Clemence Dane Cup/Pat Garrod Cup was originally donated by Clemence Dane when she was Life President. It was re-introduced in 1974 to celebrate the Society's eightieth birthday. The name of Pat Garrod was added to commemorate and honour this long-serving Secretary and Editor, following her death in 1982.

- The Theodora Roscoe/Vera Brittain Cup links two unforgettable pioneers of the Society, who did so much for it in earlier days; Theodora Roscoe who died in 1964 and Vera Brittain who died in 1970. The cup is beautiful and its provenance is linked to a legacy which originally provided a book token prize to be awarded on Country Members' Day in 1962.

- The John Walter Salver. Any member who has won the SWWJ John Walter silver salver for journalism may have wondered about the provenance of this benefactor. John Walter was the fifth person in this mighty newspaper dynasty. As the proprietor and Editor of *The Times*, he offered his patronage in the late 1920s and was a steadfast and trusted friend of the Society. His original intention in offering the trophy that bears his name was to raise funds for post-war charities, and so it was that he presented the salver in an article competition in the 1947 Open Annual Literary Festival. Elizabeth Pozzy won the 2008 John Walter Salver.

- The Lady Longford Award. Following the death in 2002 of the Society's former Life President Lady Longford, an annual Poetry Competition is held in her memory. This was awarded in 2009 to Alison Chisholm.

- The Christmas Competition. This annual competition usually has a festive theme and has, in past years, been awarded for poetry, fiction and articles.

- Scholarships. Additionally, two scholarships for places at the Weekend School are awarded in memory of Joyce Grenfell and Sir Harry Brittain.

The trophies, with their provenance and photographs of the originating Society benefactors, are kept at Chawton House, in Hampshire, following presentation at award ceremonies. Chawton House is the former home of Jane Austen's brother. Competition winners receive a certificate as a memento with their cheque.

# eleven

# *Drama*

## Stage and Screen

The launch of the Society during the 1890s coincided with the introduction of the cinema. From the start of this incredible innovation, we see that drama has played an important part in the lives and careers of many writers and actors. Fortunately, some of the pioneering members had links with the theatre and famous actor-managers of the time. Although not a member of the Society, the famous actress Sarah Bernhardt's name often appeared on invitation lists of 'At Home' evenings. She was a friend of President of the time, Millicent, Duchess of Sutherland. When Sarah's childhood friend, Mrs Leon Rueff, came to give a talk in 1947, she said that the 'Divine Sarah' had suffered greatly from stage fright all her life. She was also distrustful of banks and carried her fortune around in her capacious chamois-leather bag.

Entertaining fellow members in the early days of the Society was as popular as it is today. In 1911, playlets, musical evenings and recitations were put on by members and one, in particular, the *Nursing Masque* written by the famous Mrs Bedford Fenwick, was held at the Connaught Rooms in the city. Described as a 'striking pageant', its purpose was to raise funds to support the Bill for the State Registration of Trained Nurses.

Winifred Ashton (Clemence Dane) was born in 1888. She was a playwright, poet, sculptor, and actress (known as Diana Cortis) and certainly become one of the Society's most active members, eventually becoming President. She was regarded as one of the most successful playwrights in London during the 1920s. Her play, *A Bill of Divorcement*, caused a sensation at the time, and was later made into a film. She had two plays running simultaneously in London theatres. The July 1946 edition of *The Woman Journalist* notes that Clemence was in Hollywood discussing the filming of *Perfect Strangers* in which she received top credit.

During and after the Second World War, the Society began play-reading sessions at regular intervals, assisted by professional actors, producers and directors who often attended. These were friends of Clemence Dane and Joyce Grenfell. In January 1947, scriptwriting was the theme for a competition to be performed by Ruth Draper, Joyce Grenfell,

Joyce Grenfell with Lord Willis, playwright, and
SWWJ Secretary, Pat Garrod.

Jeanne de Casalis, Ivy St Helier and Mabel
Constandurous. Although Joyce was working
with Noel Coward on his revue, *Sigh No
More,* she found time to come along to the
Society's play-reading session that took place
in November.

Spring 1948 was exciting for one of the
play-reading enthusiasts. Doreen Simpson's
play *The Sparks Fly Upward* was put on at
the Q Theatre in Kew. Professional actor
Rachel Kempson starred in the leading role
with Hugh Latimer and Aubrey Dextor. This
Drama Group, which continued for several
years, went on to see much of their members'
work performed professionally.

Pat Garrod, Society Secretary and later Editor of *The Woman Journalist,* was winning
awards for her one-act plays from the early 1950s. Her earlier friendship with leading
actors and tutors at London's acting schools meant a fascinating turnover of speakers.
The famous Miss Mary Gertrude Pickersgill, who then ran the London School of
Dramatic Art ensured a packed house at the September 1956 gathering when she lectured
on the art of mime and stage production. The Society has since enjoyed a warm fellowship
with RADA from the time it opened in London's Gower Street. Full circle was reached
in February 2004 when the SWWJ Drama Group returned to the Acting Room for their
rehearsed reading workshop at RADA theatre. The team now use the Helios Centre.

Both Joyce Grenfell and Pat Garrod had a wide circle of friends and acquaintances from
the world of stage and screen. This meant that *The Woman Journalist* was always brimming
with articles from some of the greatest names in film and theatre. So, from the 1950s,
readers enjoyed the literary thoughts of everyone from Dame Sybil Thorndike, Lord (Ted)
Willis, Chaim Topol, Spike Milligan, Rosemary Nicholls and many connected with the
acting world.

Joyce Grenfell's film appearances are legendary. Her debut, in 1943, was a small part in
the propaganda film *The Lamp Still Burns,* playing a lecturer on blood donation, starring
Rosamund John. This was followed by *This Demi-Paradise* starring Laurence Olivier and
Margaret Rutherford, and so it went on with larger film parts such as *The Happiest Days
of your Life* in 1950, starring Alastair Sim, a film that remains a great classic. *Genevieve*
followed in 1953, *The Belles of St Trinian's* in 1954 and many more including, in 1964,
*The Americanisation of Emily* – all timeless classics. What is remarkable is that during the
Second World War, she was touring with ENSA, working in hospitals, writing reviews,
poetry and features for the radio. An amazing woman.

'A woman for all seasons' describes Jean McConnell, former Chairman and now
Vice-President. Jean has been a Society member since 1989 and was already well-known

Vice-President Jean McConnell, Jennie Lisney and Brian Forbes, the actor and film producer.

in the theatre, radio and film world as writer, producer, director and actor touring with the Glyndebourne Theatre Company. She appeared at the early Bath and Edinburgh Festivals and on television. With the success of her first television play, she followed this with dozens of single plays, serials and films. Married with a new baby, she began writing a television play and was, in fact, the first woman writer to do so. Her play, *Haul for the Shore*, was highly successful and she was given three separate productions. Ten years later, this was voted one of the best twelve plays seen on BBC television. Subsequently, including radio and stage versions, it has been produced at least 3,000 times. She followed this by creating further plays for the BBC including *Dr Finlay's Casebook*, and dozens of single plays, serials and films.

While working on a television adaptation of her radio series, *The Emptages*, she was invited by producers Frank Muir and Denis Norden to join the Screenwriters Guild, which is now the Writers' Guild of Great Britain. Thereafter, she served on its Executive Committee, Books Committee and Awards Committee. She served six years on the board of the Churchill Theatre, Bromley, and has been three times on the Management Committee of the Crime Writers Association.

Nina Bawden, SWWJ President, is the author of more than forty books. *Carrie's War* is probably the best known, published in 1973, followed by the wonderful *The Peppermint Pig* in 1975, two stories for children that have attained the status of modern classics. *The Peppermint Pig* won the Guardian Award for Children's Fiction in 1975, and both books were made into children's television serials by the BBC during the 1970s. *Carrie's War*, which is on the National Curriculum and was filmed again by the BBC in 2009, is a retelling of Nina's experiences as a child evacuee in the Second World War. *Circles of Deceit*, shortlisted for the Booker Prize, was made into a film for BBC 2. Her most recent book, *Dear Austen*, was written following the tragic death of her husband Austen Kark in the Potters Bar train crash in 2002.

Over the years, numerous members have seen their work appear first on the printed page, and then have had the joy of experiencing it professionally produced in the theatre and on film. Multi-talented Benita Cullingford is Council Hon. Treasurer but is also an author, actor, and scriptwriter. She has taught speech and drama for the London Academy of Music and Dramatic Art and adjudicates at drama festivals. Benita has written many articles and is the author of three non-fiction books. She is known as the 'chimney sweeps' historian'. Benita has written three short films and her first feature film, *Portia's Penguin*, was short-listed in the Screenwriters' Festival, Cheltenham 2007, and has been optioned by Unital Films (UK). Benita is working on a final draft of the script with a consultant from Euroscript. Benita is a member of the Books' Committee (Writers' Guild of Great Britain).

Past Chairman Mary Rensten has been a journalist and teacher for much of her professional life. She has been a regular contributor to *The Lady* magazine over the last twenty years. Mary has been writing and producing plays for amateur theatre for many years.

It seems that writing and drama go hand in hand and throughout the years, the SWWJ has attracted many actors. Present Overseas Liaison Officer, Phyllis Ellis-Franks, has written for most of her adult life, but started her career as an actor under the name Tricia Ellis. She has held her Equity card for over fifty years and still treads the boards. Why she seemed so familiar when she joined the Society was that during the 1960s, she made more than thirty television commercials, appearing in advertisements for Heinz Baked Beans and more memorably as the 'Fairy Liquid Mum'.

Another member whose career began in film and theatre is Fiona Kendall, whose grandmother was the famous music hall star, Marie Kendall. Fiona's cousins Kay Kendall (star of *Genevieve*) and Cavan Kendall, were well-known stage and television actors. Kay and Joyce Grenfell were friends, having met on the set of *Genevieve*.

*Left* SWWJ Overseas Liaison Officer Phyllis Ellis-Franks, with George Chisholm, on stage during her acting days.

*Below* Member Fiona Kendall-Lane in her glamorous film star days. (Photograph by kind permission of F. Kendall-Lane)

The Drama Group meet in London at the St Bride's Institute, February 2009. Organised by Associate Member Martin Cort, back row, fourth from right.

Fiona attended the Italia Conti Stage School, toured in repertory and became well-known in the first ever live video-linked television quiz show, *Quest*. Fiona appeared in numerous productions including *Dracula*, three *Carry On* films and what is now the cult film, *Psychomania*. She has had several novels published to much acclaim, together with short stories, articles and sagas. In 2005, Fiona won the SWWJ's coveted award, the John Walter Salver, for her story set in the Scottish Highlands. Fiona became Council Vice-Chair in 2006.

In 2004, a decision was made to invite men to join the Society as Associate Members. Martin Cort, who joined in 2005, is an actor, director and producer. Since 2000, the list of his professionally performed work has grown and the success of his play adaptations includes many award-winning scripts. Martin researches national television in Japan and has organised numerous drama days for the Society in London.

Helen Shay has had several plays staged in new writing festivals. One was at the International Women Playwrights' Conference in the Philippines in 2003 and her work has appeared at the Edinburgh Fringe and in her local theatre in Harrogate. In 2006, she won the Joyce Grenfell Award for a radio play which has since been broadcast on local radio. Helen is also well-known for her prize-winning poetry.

Carolyn Pertwee turned from acting to writing and almost immediately received a television commission for her comedy drama series *Rosie and Dud*. Carolyn's Radio 4 play *The Beautiful Couple* staring Julia McKenzie and Ronald Pickup was the choice of the day in all national press. Her short plays have been performed at the Soho Theatre, Hackney Empire and the Royal National Institute.

June Walker reckons that her membership of the Society has contributed to her success as a playwright. June's one-act comedy *The Middlewood Manor Affair* was published shortly after switching from short story writing, and she is a regular contributor to the Drama Days at London's Helios Centre.

# twelve

# *Poetry*

## Poetry matters

When Mr Snell Wood created the Society of Woman Journalists so long ago, newspaperwomen were the principal group of writers with whom he was most concerned. But, by the end of the nineteenth century, writers of many other genres were applying for membership. Some were poets and one of the best known at the time was Alice Meynell (1847-1922). Her family home was in Barnes, London. Alice's father had been a friend of Charles Dickens and as a child, Alice had met and mixed with many eminent writers of the day.

Alice began writing poetry as a small child and her work was admired by her father's famous visitors. Her first important collection of poems, *Preludes,* received great critical acclaim from many of the leading writers of the time, including George Eliot, John Ruskin and Dante Gabriel Rossetti. Her reputation for worthy poetry was considerable during her lifetime. She was nominated twice when the position of Poet Laureate became vacant, first in 1895 and again in 1913.

Endorsements by Rudyard Kipling, Alfred Lord Tennyson and G.K. Chesterton failed to help her elevation. The government feared that conferring such an honour upon women could be seen as a victory for the Suffragettes. The political situation raging at the time spoiled her chances, as militant Suffragettes were causing damage to London buildings. In 1913, Robert Seymour Bridges became Poet Laureate. Alice's work is widely read today and one of her poems, 'She walks – The Lady of my Delight (The Shepherdess)' appears in many school anthologies

Although, from the early days of the Society poets saw their work published in leading poetry collections, journals and daily newspapers of the time, from an historical viewpoint it was Society Patron Sir Harry Brittain who can claim to have been the first to 'recite' his poetry into the shiny, black instrument newly-installed by the London Telephone Company – the year was 1879 and Sir Harry was a cheeky four-year-old.

Friendly help was always evident from notable members such as the distinguished poet Mrs Arthur Hughes (Mary Winter Were). In March 1935, the Royal Chapel of the Savoy

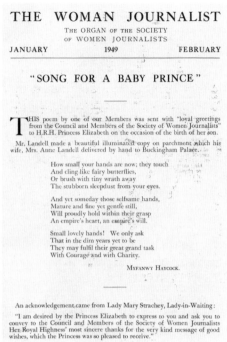

THE WOMAN JOURNALIST
THE ORGAN OF THE SOCIETY
OF WOMEN JOURNALISTS

JANUARY         1949         FEBRUARY

### "SONG FOR A BABY PRINCE"

THIS poem by one of our Members was sent with "loyal greetings from the Council and Members of the Society of Women Journalists" to H.R.H. Princess Elizabeth on the occasion of the birth of her son.

Mr. Landell made a beautiful illuminated copy on parchment which his wife, Mrs. Anne Landell delivered by hand to Buckingham Palace.

> How small your hands are now; they touch
> And cling like fairy butterflies,
> Or brush with tiny wrath away
> The stubborn sleepdust from your eyes.
>
> And yet someday those selfsame hands,
> Mature and fine yet gentle still,
> Will proudly hold within their grasp
> An empire's heart, an empire's will.
>
> Small lovely hands!  We only ask
> That in the dim years yet to be
> They may fulfil their great grand task
> With Courage and with Charity.
>
> MYFANWY HAYCOCK.

An acknowledgement came from Lady Mary Strachey, Lady-in-Waiting:

"I am desired by the Princess Elizabeth to express to you and ask you to convey to the Council and Members of the Society of Women Journalists Her Royal Highness' most sincere thanks for the very kind message of good wishes, which the Princess was so pleased to receive."

*Left*  Alice Meynell, no ordinary poet, etc. (Photograph by kind permission of the National Portrait Gallery)

*Right*  Poet Myfanwy Haycock's poem dedicated to Prince Charles.

was the venue organised by the Poetry Society for her to read her new poem, 'The Mystical Story of Glastonbury'. She was chosen to write Rudyard Kipling's obituary following his death in 1936. The piece appeared in the Spring edition of *The Woman Journalist*.

Although one Council member, the Editor-in-Chief of *Weldon's,* Julia Cairns, was also writing her lovely prose and verse during the early 1930s, it was not until March 1937 that her anthologies *Stardust* and *More Stardust*, were published by Weldon's Press.

War changed every aspect of the writing world. Emotions during these fraught, disturbed years inspired poets to create some of their finest work. Society members were seeing their poetry published in *The Lady, Strand Magazine, John O'London's Weekly* and other periodicals. In the early 1940s, membership included the well-known poets Carla Hacker (née Lanyon Lanyon) and Theodora Roscoe. Members received Christmas cards that year containing the famous poem composed by Mary Winter Were entitled 'Deo Gratias'.

Poetry Quizzes were popular and Theodora Roscoe was usually appointed Question Master at these gatherings. Dora Camm and Veronica Mileson were able supporters. Another superb poet was Clemence Dane (later to become our Life President) who achieved tremendous success in many areas of writing, including drama, art and all forms of literature.

Myfanwy Haycock's poetry became well-known and when Prince Charles was born on 14 November 1948, she composed her 'Song for a Baby Prince' which was sent to

Buckingham Palace by the Society's Secretary and was well-received by the then Princess Elizabeth. This was published in the January 1949 edition of *The Woman Journalist*.

Poetry workshops were usually well attended and the work emerging led to the publication of many fine anthologies. The Poetry section within the first Literary Festival in 1947 attracted hundreds of entries. In the Spring edition of *The Woman Journalist* that year, the newly-created 'Poetry Corner' invited members to send their work in for publication.

Dr Marie Stopes (1880-1958), famous throughout the world as a birth control campaigner and author of many non-fiction books which sold in their millions, had been a member for many years. She loved writing poetry and produced several volumes of verse during the last years of her life. One collection entitled *Joy and Verity* was published by the Hogarth Press.

In March 1949, members flocked to Stationers' Hall to hear Ruth Pitter (1897-1992), one of the greatest twentieth-century British poets. She later became the first woman to receive the Queen's Gold Medal for Poetry in 1955, and was appointed a CBE in 1979 to honour her many contributions to English literature. In 1974, she had been named a 'Companion of Literature', the highest honour given by the Royal Society of Literature.

Following the death of Queen Mary in 1953, member Ada Jackson's poem 'Princess Mary' was published in several northern newspapers. In May 1954, Theodora Roscoe's

A wonderful poetry meeting in March 2009 arranged by Poetry Advisor Doris Corti (front row, fourth from left) and Poetry Representative Anita Marie Sackett (front row, far right).

collection *St Alban's & Other Poems* was selling well. At the time of Theodora's death in 1962, her poetry and prose had become extremely well-known.

The Poetry Society, established in 1909, often invited Society members to their special events and supplied speakers for Society poetry meetings. The adjudicator for the Poetry Class for the November 1954 Literary Festival was the then Poet Laureate, Sir John Masefield.

'Poetry' was the title of Dame Edith Sitwell's talk at the hall of Church House, Westminster, in May 1957. This memorable event came under the auspices of the 1957 Herman Ould Memorial Lecture organised by the English Centre of International PEN. Our Patron, Dr C.V. Wedgwood CBE chaired the lecture and many members filled the hall.

In 1962, the Society's intrepid Editor, Pat Garrod, paid a visit to Cecil Day Lewis (1904-1972), then Poet Laureate. The great poet said that he had always wanted to write poetry and started as an eight-year-old. He suggested that poets needed a lot of solitude, though personally once started, he could write a poem in a room filled with talking people. Mr Day Lewis said that during the war, people turned to poetry because in times of destruction they wanted permanence.

In 1966, May Badman (née Ivimy) joined the Society. Born in Greenwich in 1912, May has written poetry for most of her life. She and Joan Rice founded Ver Poets in St Albans. May served on Council as Poetry Representative and Advisor and has also worked on the Executive Council of the Poetry Society. May's recollections of the past remain sharp and her remarkable output of verse is incorporated in many wonderful collections, the last of which was *A Life in Poetry*, which was enhanced by beautiful line drawings by May's husband, Ray.

Joyce Grenfell – destined to become President of the Society in later years – had written poetry from a very young age and her first earnings were from her poetry. She went on writing verse all her life. Many of her clever, affectionate and sometimes acerbic verses first appeared in *Punch, The Observer, The Christian Science Monitor* and *Country Life.*

Joyce and Sir John Betjeman were good friends and enjoyed each other's company. They were delighted to be asked to compile a poetry recital programme during the early 1970s. In her autobiography *In Pleasant Places,* Joyce tells us that the work was carried out partly by telephone and partly by letter, but best of all in sessions at Elm Park Gardens. 'He used to arrive carrying an old-fashioned flat straw bag of the kind meant for fish, bulging with poetry books'. They would spend whole afternoons reading poetry to each other. They called one of their programmes *Innocence and the World* and both enjoyed each other's poetry and company.

## Poetry Day

13 October 1981 at the Old Town Hall Arts Centre, Hemel Hempstead, was a red-letter day for members who came to the Society's first ever Poetry Day. Organised by Jean Marian Stevens, a warm welcome was given to Roger Burford Mason, the poetry editor and publisher who was guest speaker, along with Alec Reid from the BBC Drama Department. This was a special day to remember where old and new friends met.

Vice-President Jean Marian Stevens, who will celebrate her sixtieth year with the Society in 2010.

Many of our poets are listed in the various editions of the *International Who's Who in Poetry* and *The Poets' Encyclopaedia*. These include Susan Skinner, who joined the Society in April 1993. She was encouraged and inspired by Ursula Fanthorpe at an Arvon Course. She went on to publish two collections with Headland, poems in a number of anthologies and magazines. Susan won the Julia Cairns Salver four times and was privileged to have met Julia Cairns just before this wonderful poet died in December 1985.

Alison Chisholm, Doris Corti and Peggy Poole are all poetry columnists with *Writers' News*, each of whose own work has brought them nationwide recognition. Doris Corti has held the position of SWWJ Poetry Advisor since 1986. Fay Marshall, Maryann Foster, Philippa Lawrence, Daphne Schiller and lately Anita Marie Sackett have all been the Poetry Representative on Council. Each has brought their unique expertise to this very special job. Fay Marshall runs the Poetry Critique project. Anita Marie Sackett is a talented teacher who specialises in children's poetry, but whose name is well-known in many disparate areas of writing. Her work has been published internationally.

In 2008, former Council Poetry Representative Philippa Lawrence was asked to take part in a collaboration between 'poetry pf', the online poetry resource created by poet Anne

Stewart and Professor Lidia Vianu of the University of Bucharest, for her MA and PhD students to translate some of their poems into Romanian and broadcast them on Romanian national radio. Three of Philippa's poems were broadcast and can be found, with photos, through www.poetrypf.co.uk/poetrypro.html. In April 2009, two of the translators came over for a ten-day-tour which started with a reading in London in which Philippa took part, and ended at the Romanian Cultural Institute.

SWWJ poets have been at the forefront of the increasing interest in poetry, whether in local and national radio, television or 'performance poetry'. Among the numerous talented poets the Society

Member Fay Marshall, who won the Poetry Competition (among many other awards for poetry over the years). Poetry Judge Morgan Kenney joined members at their Weekend Conference in Egham in 2004.

Philippa Lawrence (second from left) with friends from the Romanian National Broadcasting Corporation at the Romanian Embassy, London. (Photograph courtesy of Philippa Lawrence)

has been fortunate to know are Arda Lacey, Brenda Whincup, Tessa Nelson-Humphries, Val Tigwell, Beryl Cross (former Chairman), Barbara Rennie, Val Waters, Finola Holiday, Alfa and Dorothy Pope and, of course, Jean Marian Stevens.

## Anthologies

The Society has published several anthologies created by its members, usually linked to anniversaries: *Valuable Things*, 1975, *Candles and Lamps*, 1979, which included poems by Joyce Grenfell, and *A Mirror to our Day,* 1984. *Animal Cavalcade* was another excellent collection of poems. To celebrate the Millennium, a slim anthology, *Tessellation*, was published which was a mosaic of prize-winning poetry and prose from earlier competitions.

# thirteen

# *Periodicals*

Write, be published – be paid! This was the aim of journalists and authors in 1894, the year the Society of Women Journalists was created. Periodicals for 'the women at home' were becoming increasingly popular. Members skilled in writing articles enjoyed seeing their work published within the pages of *The Tatler*, founded in 1709. *Punch* started in 1841, *The Lady* magazine in 1890, whose Editor Rita Shell was Society Treasurer, and *The Gentlewoman,* which made its debut in 1885 and was owned by Joseph Snell Wood. As an experienced editor of several national dailies, Joseph had a fair idea of what the Victorian upper-class thinking woman wanted to read.

Periodicals aimed at women were nothing new. They had been published for centuries. John Dunton, a London bookseller, seems to have started the ball rolling in 1693 when he bravely published *The Ladies' Mercury*, aimed specifically at 'the fair sex'. Dunton assured his readers, 'We shall be ready to answer all questions you shall vouchsafe to send us'. So began the first 'Agony' column. He was as good as his word. The paper teemed with answers to 'all the most nice and curious questions concerning love, marriage behaviour, dress and humour of the female sex, whether virgins, wives or widows' and the most intimate problems were aired in its pages with a forthrightness typical of an age which was bawdy, lusty and uninhibited.

In 1709, *The Tatler* was launched and, except for a few years during the 1960s, has been continuously published. But in those early days of the eighteenth century, the educated men and women alike enjoyed the tittle-tattle of this journal in their new-fangled coffee-houses that had sprung up around London's Fleet Street. *The Tatler* is, of course, Britain's oldest extant magazine. During the 1770s, almanacs, diaries and two-page 'broadsides' aimed at educated women were printed and distributed liberally in drawing rooms and social gatherings. Towards end of the century emerged the beginning of the women's periodical press with the launch of *La Belle Assemblee, The Lady's Monthly Museum, The Female Friend, The Ladies' Cabinet,* and many others. The twentieth-century lady could take her choice as she was regaled with news and notes on cookery, fashion, etiquette, literary criticism and gardening. The growth of women's periodicals continued during the early years of the twentieth century, since there was a 'feminine audience… ready and waiting… to patronise enterprises directed to women'.

## *The Lady*

This periodical played a vital part in the lives of Society members from the start. *The Lady* was launched on Thursday 19 February 1885, by the politician and journalist, Thomas Gibson Bowles (1869-1922), a charismatic man, already the proprietor of the first *Vanity Fair* magazine, for which he wrote many of the articles himself. His new 'journal for gentlewomen' enjoyed brisk sales during the age of epoch-making invention of the Linotype printing machines which were then being adopted by *The New York Times* and being introduced into London newspaper printing offices.

The world of feminism was stirring; women had taken up bicycling, began thinking of careers and the 'New Woman', a term coined by the Society's President of the time, Madame Sarah Grand (1854-1943), who was to play such an important role as a pioneer of the Society, was beginning to make an appearance. Life was changing and this was reflected in members' writing.

*The Lady's* advance publicity stated, 'to look beautiful is one of the first duties of a lady', to which Charles L. Dodgson (Lewis Carroll) took exception. This was a period of modest reticence on the subject of beauty. The first issue of *The Lady* sold 2,361 copies – there were thirty-six pages, nearly all illustrated, and the actual page size was considerably larger than that of today. The price was 6*d*, which was soon reduced to 3*d*. Readers became familiar with the layout, which rarely changed. The front pages consisted of columns mainly of 'Exchange and Sale', 'an advantage offered by no other journal', which was followed by 'Employment – for the purpose of bringing employers and those ladies who wish to be employed together in a manner never before attempted.'

The strong link between *The Lady* and the SWWJ was due to the unforgettable Rita Shell, who was appointed Editor in 1895 by Thomas Bowles. It was she who introduced so many interesting editorials and championed worthwhile women's causes – such as improving conditions for nurses and urging women to stand for election to their local Board of Guardians, among other social projects. Rita's salary on appointment was £7 a week. It's hard to credit that the editorial staff of four, at times reduced to three, and on one occasion to one, could have produced a magazine of such quality with up to fifty-two editorial pages, increased in special numbers to seventy-eight.

Not many people realise that Rita Shell, on her appointment, was the mother of four young boys and had been governess to Mr Bowles' young family when his wife died in 1888. His eldest daughter, Sydney, married the Hon. David Mitford, later Lord Reisdale, and together they produced their famous family of seven daughters and one son, David.

*The Lady* has prospered under four generations of Bowles' proprietors through its 125 years' unbroken publication. Rita's editorship continued until 1925. Upon hearing of her death in 1951, Theodora Roscoe commented:

> Her life-long work for our Society was carried out with a deep sense of the highest aims, and of the standard she wished it to maintain. To some, this standard seems too exacting for modern trends, but it is to Rita Shell and other pioneer women journalists and writers, that we owe the moulding of the character of our Society.

In 2009, *The Lady* once again underwent editorial changes. With a fresh, modern update, new contributors and the ever-popular 'Classified Advertisements' positioned towards the end of the journal, this magazine goes from strength to strength.

## People's Friend

This magazine has long been a favourite with older Society members and many have contributed their work to D.C. Thomson, the publisher. Its editorial office has remained in Dundee, Scotland, since its launch in 1869. Their tagline, 'The famous story magazine', continues. The magazine's geographical location is reflected in a general bias toward Scottish readers and the main front cover image is invariably a painting of a picturesque location somewhere in the British Isles. Readers can also buy prints of these pictures.

## John O'London's Weekly

From its launch in 1919, *John O' London's Weekly* was, in its time, one of the most widely read periodicals. It was a favourite of Society members and was regularly advertised in *The Woman Journalist*. Several members, including Joyce Elsden, contributed to its pages. Readers enjoyed its thoughtful articles that touched all manner of lively topics, from the editor's own observations to features on modern science, trends in art and literature, examination of the 'new theatre', national developments in Europe and much more. During its time, it was considered to be the leading literary magazine in the British Empire. Named after the pen name of one of its early editors, *John O'London's Weekly* demonstrated the best writing by great names and by young unknowns. It ran a section on English grammar and word usage, recommended good books and enjoyed a steady circulation of 80,000. Society members, such as Dame Rebecca West and Ivy Compton-Burnett, were among its contributors, as were Winston Churchill, Arnold Bennett, Max Beerbohm, and W. Somerset Maugham. During the Second World War, newsprint restrictions and staff leaving to enter the services cut the magazine's circulation to 50,000, and sadly it never recovered.

## Time & Tide

Lady Margaret Rhondda was elected as Society Vice-President after the Second World War. She founded the literary magazine *Time & Tide* in 1920, to which many of her fellow members contributed. Lady Rhondda took over editorship from Helen Archdale in 1926. Contributors to the magazine included Vera Brittain, Winifred Holtby, Virginia Woolf, Storm Jameson, Charlotte Despard, Emmeline Pankhurst, Eleanor Rathbone, Olive Schreiner, Margaret Rebecca West, Rose Macaulay, Naomi Mitchison, Helena Swanwick, Ellen Wilkinson, Ethel Smyth, D.H. Lawrence, George Bernard Shaw, Robert Graves and George Orwell. The journal did not sell well, and Lady Rhondda lost a great deal of money over the journal's latter years, ceasing publication in 1977.

Dame Rebecca West was a Council member during the 1950s. (Photograph courtesy of Virago)

## *The Stage* Newspaper

Among Mr Snell Wood's friends was the Editor of *The Stage* (published under the title *The Stage Directory – a London and Provincial Theatrical Advertiser*) which had been launched on 1 February 1880 at a cost of 3*d* and consisting of twelve pages.

Publication was monthly until 25 March 1881, when the first weekly edition was produced. At the same time, the name was shortened to *The Stage* and the publication numbering restarted at No. 1. The publication was a joint venture between founding Editor Charles Lionel Carson and Business Manager Maurice Comerford, and operated from offices opposite the Theatre Royal, Drury Lane.

*The Stage* has, from the Society's earliest days, played an important part in the lives of many members interested in film and theatre. Undercutting their rivals, Carson and Comerford dropped the price of the paper to 1*d* and it was soon the only remaining title in its field. Upon the death, in 1937, of Charles Carson's son, Lionel, who had assumed the joint role of Managing Director and Editor, control passed to the Comerford family. In 1959, *The Stage* was relaunched as *The Stage and Television Today*, incorporating a pull-out supplement dedicated to broadcasting news and features. Great changes have inevitably taken place over the last fifty years but *The Stage*, now completely in the technological world, encompassing websites and blogs, still enjoys its leading position after 130 years of publication.

# Good Housekeeping

Another favourite journal in which members' work appeared was the English edition of the American home monthly *Good Housekeeping*. This appeared in March 1922 and the editorial staff set out to sell the magazine as an all round homemaking service. It provided up to date information on food, goods and services. Justifying this home approach, its Editor wrote:

> Any keen observer of the times cannot have failed to notice that we are on the threshold of a great feminine awakening. Apathy and levity are alike giving place to a wholesome and intelligent interest in the affairs of life, and above all, in the home. We believe that the time is ripe for a great new magazine which shall worthily meet the needs of the housekeeping woman of today.

The magazine was conceived to teach middle-class women how to run their homes, especially after the First World War when the days of domestic help suddenly came to an end. Many had to undertake culinary tasks for the first time, since one of the effects of the war had been to deplete the number of women willing to enter domestic service, diverting them instead to industrial work.

Domestic management suddenly became an 'art' and *Good Housekeeping* was their 'bible'. Society members were not slow in sending in their work. The Editor required 'articles on topics of interest to intelligent women', which still stands today. 'Housekeeping is a business and to attempt to run it on other than a business basis is simply courting disaster. A budget is essential' wrote the two principals of *Good Housekeeping's* school of home management in Clifton in the fourth issue. As proof of the seriousness of *Good Housekeeping's* determination to get things right, the *Good Housekeeping* Institute was opened in 1924 with a team of women creating and testing recipes for inclusion in the journal. *Good Housekeeping* also ran a restaurant in Oxford Street, a training school for home economists and, later on, a wartime meals centre where meals could be purchased.

Another Society member, author Rose Macaulay, was an early contributor to *Good Housekeeping*. Her features were always thoughtful and she would write about 'Problems for the Citizen', as she did in 1923.

Helena Normanton BA, England's first woman barrister and a Society Vice-Chairman, also contributed. She wrote numerous articles for *Good Housekeeping,* one famous feature in 1924 was entitled 'The Adulteration of Food', which told us that 'we had more than one thousand chances of being poisoned each year of our lives'. Another she entitled 'Super women in business', published in 1926, wouldn't seem out of place in 2010. Her feature on 'Breach of Promise' in 1928 asks, 'Is compensation on this score an anachronism in these days of emancipated women?'

One Society Patron, Mrs John Buchan (Lady Susan Tweedsmuir), who had done so much to help fellow journalists, wrote regularly for *Good Housekeeping*. Although it wasn't until 2004 that men were finally admitted to the Society as 'Associates', many male writers such as Beverley Nichols, Godfrey Winn, Noel Coward and others, contributed both to *The Woman Journalist* magazine, as well as being published by *Good Housekeeping*.

## General Magazines

The women's magazine industry, like so many other businesses, was frozen by the Second World War. The government allocated a paper rationing system, which operated on a pre-war average usage. The magazines that survived the advent of the war had no freedom to expand, either in circulation or issue size.

During the war, reading matter was hard to obtain and then of such a limited size that everything printed enjoyed a ready market. Women on the Home Front and in the services mopped up the magazines, which hit the bookstalls. In 1946-47 there were about thirty leading weekly and monthly magazines on the market. Many titles had not survived the war.

*Woman's* circulation, however, had just hit the magic 1 million in 1946 and its arch-rival, *Woman's Own*, stood at 700,000. Mary Grieve was at the helm of *Woman* and James Drawbell was at Newnes' *Woman's Own*. Current member Elizabeth Hart worked for George Newnes and Jean Bowden was, during the 1960s, Assistant Editor at *Woman's Own*.

Magazines were the subject of Mrs Gerald Legge's talk at Stationers' Hall in April 1955. As the youngest London City Councillor at that time, she spoke about the importance of women journalists and their value as the brains, as well as the eyes, ears and mouth of the public. Journalists had it in their power not only to mould public opinion, but to fashion taste. The women's magazines brought colour and glamour into countless lives and deserved great praise for the things they taught. As the daughter of the novelist Barbara Cartland and the future Countess Spencer, Mrs Legge had great praise for the women journalists of the fifties.

# fourteen
# *The War Years*

## The Boer War

'As soon as war is declared, it will be impossible to hold back the poets.' (Jean Giraudoux, 1882-1944). Although Lady Sarah Wilson, aunt to Winston Churchill and President of the Society in the early years of the twentieth century, was known to enjoy writing poetry, her claim to fame was as a journalist. Born in 1865, Lady Sarah wrote several books about her remarkable life in which she described her numerous experiences of great happiness and deep anxiety during her time in the theatre of war in South Africa's Transvaal.

Her husband, Lieutenant-Colonel Gordon Chesney Wilson, had moved to Mafeking at the start of the Boer War. He was Aide-de-Camp to Colonel Robert Baden-Powell, Commanding Officer at Mafeking.

Baden-Powell suggested Sarah should leave Mafeking for her own safety after the Boers threatened to storm the British garrison. Sarah was later to write about the madcap adventure in the company of her maid, travelling through the South African countryside. Captured by the enemy, she was returned to the town in exchange for a horse thief being held there. Although untrained as a journalist, Lady Sarah soon gained a huge following among *Daily Mail* readers back in England who appreciated her matter-of-fact writing style.

Lady Sarah Wilson, former President of the Society, an extraordinary journalist working for the *Daily Mail*.

*Left* Vera Brittain in her VAD uniform. Her life and diaries have been the subject of many books and films. (With thanks to McMaster University Library Hamilton, Ontario)

*Right* Stationers' Hall, this ancient, beautiful building, was a favourite venue for members meetings for many years. It was bombed during the Second World War and has subsequently been rebuilt.

# The First World War

The picture famously showing the Kaiser on the front page of the *Daily Mail* entitled *The Sword is thrust into my hand* shows the date of 3 August 1914. The people cheering so lustily in London could have no idea of what this terrible war to end all wars would do to them and their menfolk. Life President Vera Brittain was later to write so poignantly about the First World War in her best-selling book *Testament of Youth*. The action was so much closer to home than the conflict in South Africa fifteen years earlier and involved millions of young men.

The women closest to the front line, on some occasions even working among the men in the trenches, were the various corps and groups of nurses. Among the nursing groups that are remembered for their noble work in France are the Territorial Force Nursing Service, First Aid Nursing Yeomanry (FANY), Naval Nursing Services, Red Cross and Voluntary Aid Detachment (VAD), whose headquarters were set up in London by another of our Presidents, Lady Violet Astor. She and Lady Ampthill championed the purchase of the New Cavendish Club at Marble Arch. This is now the Society's venue for many of our special occasions in modern times. Books, diary notes and letters from the First World War formed the basis of many of members' publications during this time.

# Press Coverage

In October 1915, Society journalists covered the memorial service for Edith Cavell, the British nurse working in German-occupied Brussels. She had helped hundreds of Allied soldiers to escape. Her execution received significant sympathetic press coverage. First cousin to this remarkable woman was a staunch Society Council member, the journalist

Fanny Strutt-Cavell (1869-1929) who joined Joseph Snell Wood's original Council in 1894. Fanny had also worked with Mr Snell Wood on *The Gentlewoman*.

Elizabeth Banks (1870-1938), one of our liveliest American journalist members, sailed for Montreal in September 1916, spending three months in Canada and the US where she went on newspaper missions connected with war work. She wrote regularly for a London daily using her pen name, Mary Mortimer Maxwell.

## The Second World War

On the first day of September 1939, Germany invaded Poland. Two days later, England was at war. The next six years – as we were to discover – were like no other and the suffering, bombing and Blitz, shortage of food, rationing and deprivation became an inescapable part of British life.

Member Kay Gilmour wrote an article for *The Woman Journalist* based on her work as a young VAD nurse in a casualty clearing station in France during the First World War. Thereafter, she roamed Europe, wrote the first guide in English to the Republic of Finland and, during the Second World War, served with the Young Women's Christian Association.

From the start, London was a dangerous place in which to live, but members continued, incongruously, to meet for their weekly tea on Thursdays, from 4.15 p.m. till 6 p.m. at their Club Rooms, whose address from 1944 was at 184-185 Temple Chambers, with more formal gatherings at Stationers' Hall. Play-reading and Brains Trusts became popular from 1942 onwards and the well-known author Mary Thomas arranged the meetings. Paper was in short supply, as was almost everything then – people wrote on anything available, even lavatory paper.

As magazine contributors know, the layout for periodicals is planned months ahead. Looking through the September 1939 magazines, strangely, there is hardly a mention of the actual outbreak of the war, although it had been on people's minds for so long. Society members such as Margaret Storm Jameson, Elizabeth Ward (Fay Inchfawn), Theodora Roscoe, Elise Sprott, Ruby M. Ayres, Mary Thomas, Ursula Bloom, Sarah Tooley and so many more continued where they had left off pre-war. They aimed their articles, poetry, essays and plays, now with a war-themed background of Make Do and Mend, learning to Dig for Victory and, indeed, becoming knowledgeable for the first time, in many cases, of how to live without servants.

A Vice-President in later years, the eminent lawyer Helena Normanton (1882-1957) was commissioned to write a series of uplifting articles for *Good Housekeeping*. Storm Jameson wrote articles in 1939 entitled *Smiling Through* about the impending war. Unlike the First World War, the Second World War came into everyone's home and by the time it was over, many dwellings had been damaged or destroyed. Families separated or shrank through conscription, evacuation or death. Many increased when others were billeted on them. No family was left unscathed. Women's magazines helped to lift spirits and offer assistance to the housewife who was often left to fight alone on the Home Front. In 1939 an extraordinary meeting of Council was called to meet at Stationers' Hall to discuss contingency plans. Within a year, the hall was bombed.

Member Joan Rice with her newly-published book *Sand in my Shoes*.

Remaining members began knitting for the troops, contributing to war funds, supplying food parcels and adopting a Merchant Ship, HM Transport *Baharistan*. Bombing raids were not the only things that the women of wartime Britain had to face. There was rationing of food, petrol and just about everything else, coupled with long queues to endure, often after a hard week's work. And there were the ubiquitous posters everywhere bearing reminders to scrimp, save and salvage. How fortunate for the archives that some members kept diaries during wartime.

Joan Rice was a teenager when war was declared. She joined the Women's Auxiliary Air Force in 1939. From Hendon and basic training, she moved to a job in Intelligence and ultimately to postings in Egypt and Palestine. At a time when diaries were supposed to be destroyed, Joan was recording her daily life in her precious chronicles. These resulted in her eventual best-selling book, published in 2006, aptly entitled *Sand in My Shoes*. In her book, we learn so much about this young woman who grew up, survived the bombing and heartache, and who after the war, went on to become a wife to Hugh, mother to three famous boys, grandmother and great-grandmother. She also returned to journalism, contributing to *The Times* when she lived in Amman, Jordan, in the 1970s.

Importantly for the Society, she was our loyal member for fifty years, before sadly passing away just after being interviewed for this book. Her eldest son, Tim, the lyricist, author and broadcaster, is a valued Patron of the Society.

The names of Joyce Grenfell and Vera Brittain appeared on the list of prospective members at the November 1943 Council meeting at Stationers' Hall. Joyce and Vera were both avid letter writers and kept journals. *Vera's Wartime Chronicles and Diary 1939-1945*, a diary as seen by a housewife living mainly in London, who was furiously writing books, letters and articles, is a remarkable testimony to this desperate time in British history.

Poet Winifred (Wyn) Parkinson arrived at Bletchley Park's code breaking centre in the spring of 1943 having been called up to the ATS. As a khaki-clad youngster, she had to undergo a stiff interview and rigorous training before joining her colleagues working in her particular hut in Block F. Enigma is a familiar word now, but then everything she did was top secret. Bletchley Park still fascinates people almost seventy years later. During her time there, Wyn remembers working for six months with Daniel Jones, the Welsh composer and boyhood friend of Dylan Thomas. Wyn feels she was inspired by Daniel and, following demob, she became a professional librarian and continued writing poetry, winning prizes and enjoying the fellowship of the SWWJ.

Noreen Riols was attached to Special Operations Executive, working alongside the famous Colonel Maurice Buckmaster at Beaulieu Manor. Noreen's personal involvement with SOE remained a secret until the official files were opened in Millennium year (see Chapter Five: 'Overseas Members').

## Keep the Flag Flying

Members were contributing their articles to wartime magazines on topics such as cooking with dried eggs, trying to feed a family on £3 a week, coping with the influx of American GIs, learning how to live with a newly-returned soldier husband and looking at repatriation. Articles on emergency beauty tricks for the morning after a sleepless night fire watching, working in a factory and similar topics were requested by editors.

From 13 April 1944, members flocked to their newly-opened Jubilee Club Rooms at Temple Chambers where Mary Thomas presided over an enormous tea urn. She wrote an amusing article for *The Woman Journalist* entitled 'A Dream Come True':

A room, a room! My kingdom for a room, was the cry in Fleet Street by the woman journalist before the war. Well, here is the room, far enough from the madding crowd, yet right in

Helen Long, Barbara Laming and Lady Muriel Brittain in Nutford House, London, in 1990.

the middle of the newspaper world. A room where [a] freelance journalist can scribble her copy, meet her friends, air her views and organise meetings or a series of discussions where progressive ideas can be put over. We are a society, not a club!

By September 1944, the Hon. Secretary was making great efforts to make personal contact with members in invaded countries. But governmental censors were returning *The Woman Journalist* with stiff messages attached asking them to refrain from sending such material through the post.

Long-standing member Verily Anderson gives younger members a wonderful chronicle of her wartime experiences in her book *Spam Tomorrow*, which outlined different aspects of the war in which she served as a FANY, driving ambulances and experiencing life as a newly-wed amid the Blitz in a top-floor London flat. When the young Verily announced her marriage, her firm, managing, generous mother threatened to stop her pocket money! Many years later, Verily is still successfully writing and seeing her work published.

During the Second World War, many of our overseas members, particularly those in Greece, France and, surprisingly, Germany managed to send reports back to London.

Helen Long's memories of the war were powerful and not easily forgotten. As a young member of the Voluntary Aid Detachment, she was posted to Haslar Hospital, Portsmouth, joining the Eighth Army medical staff in Alexandria where she nursed casualties from the Battle of El Alamein. Helen was a talented writer and her recollections were used in her autobiography of those momentous war years, *Safe Houses*. She died in 2001.

In the November 1945 issue of *The Woman Journalist*, a note was included which stated:

Let us here say thank you to Theodora Roscoe who, all through the war, has kept the monthly lectures going at Stationers' Hall. In the darkest days of raid and rumour, Mrs Roscoe steadily persuaded worthwhile speakers to come and address us in our 'front-line' HQ. And when the engagements list in *The Times* was very scanty indeed, most societies preferring to postpone their gatherings, we are proud to think that the Society of Women Journalists' lunchtime meeting was one of 'the few'. We thank again all our wartime speakers, and most of all, we thank Mrs Roscoe who brought them to us. When Hitler was no more, the Beadle of Stationers' Hall remarked upon the Society's wonderful record – we had never missed a meeting throughout the Blitz – not even one Council meeting! And Clemence Dane had the last word: 'It is a beautiful thing to see a society like ours, carrying on through the most difficult and dreadful war in our history, gamely keeping the flag flying and to see the members so fond and proud of each other.'

# fifteen

# Special Occasions

## Anniversaries

Celebrations have always been a useful catalyst for bringing members together. From the earliest meeting minutes, we know the Council of the day planned well ahead for important anniversaries and celebrations. Venues such as the Criterion restaurant, Cecil Hotel and Grosvenor Hotel in Buckingham Palace Road were popular with members at the end of the Victorian period. A special Entertainments' Committee provided exhibitions, matinees, and tea parties at the Waldorf Hotel with poetry readings and short plays to entertain members at special times. Musical and gala evenings were also arranged at London theatres and full evening dress was mandatory.

From the start, the Society had been linked to Royalty via its founder, Mr Snell Wood, and by its numerous well-connected patrons. Many famous people accepted invitations to the Society's special 'At Home' events, which were popular in Edwardian times. These were held at some of members' prestigious apartments and residences in London's best addresses. When Royalty celebrated a national event, the Society tended to follow suit. Since the 1890s, celebrations have covered Coronations, Royal weddings and special anniversaries. Sadly, as so much of the early archive is lost we have little idea of the exact details, although we do know that the Annual Dinner which celebrated the Society's first decade took place on 26 November 1905 at St Ermin's Hotel, Westminster. Mrs T.P. O'Connor, the President, proposed the health of special guest speaker, Mr Max Beerbohm Tree. Some Society members and their friends assembled to hear the celebrated Mr T.P. O'Connor MP give his illustrated lecture on 'Parliament and its Personalities'.

## Golden Anniversary, May 1944

From the collection of *The Woman Journalist* published during the early years of the Second World War, slim though they were, we know that planning for the fiftieth anniversary started early. In 1941, discussions were taking place at Stationers' Hall and although there

Golden anniversary party, 1944. Despite the war, three days were occupied with the celebrations.

was a war on at the time, plans went ahead. Clemence Dane was President at this time and Chairman was Emily Aitken. Although Stationers' Hall had been badly bombed a couple of years earlier, Council agreed this would be the venue.

A Jubilee Donation Fund was set up. Contributors were used to seeing their donation – however small – published within the magazine. Although any kind of paper was almost unobtainable, somehow Emily Aitken managed to cadge some gold paper and the fiftieth jubilee programme was a work of art. Set within its bright cover, it promised a three-day celebration in May 1944.

The first event on 23 May was a service in St Paul's Cathedral, followed by a special luncheon with messages and speeches from pioneer members. A Mansion House reception followed, presented by the Lord Mayor of London, Sir Frank Newson-Smith. Among the members, the special guests were William Redfern, the President of the Institute of Journalists, Sir Harry Brittain and Viscount Camrose, both Patrons of the society.

On 24 May, Empire Day, an exhibition of vintage clothes and memorabilia from the 1890s fascinated visitors at Stationers' Hall. The AGM was held in the afternoon. A tea party followed and the wonderful birthday cake (made by Dora Camm with members contributing their rations) was cut by Clemence Dane. Messages from veterans unable to be there made touching references to earlier members and the actress Mabel Constanduros delivered an amusing, but touching, speech. Sarah Tooley, a long-standing member, was presented with a bouquet from Clemence Dane.

On a sunny 25 May, the conference rooms of the Ministry of Information were opened to members. Here they met the Minister, the Rt Hon. Mr Brendan Bracken. Then followed a tour around the *Evening Standard* offices with a tea party at the SWJ Jubilee Clubrooms and off to Westminster Theatre to see *An Ideal Husband* by Oscar Wilde. It was a memorable few days of celebrations.

1 Mrs Humphry, 'Madge' of *Truth Magazine* fame, was one of the first magazine 'agony aunts'. (A facsimile of Mrs Humphry's book cover, by kind permission of Pryor Publications) (See page 110)

2 Phyllis Deakin. Known as a tiny human dynamo, she was Chairman of the SWWJ and created the Women's Press Club in London. She was also much involved with the evolution of the National Federation of Business & Professional Women's Clubs of Great Britain. (See page 62)

3 Penelope Wallace. A fascinating life. (Courtesy of the Wallace Collection) (See page 50)

4  SWWJ members from Dorset and Hampshire enjoy their lunch in Christchurch in 2006. (See page 43)

5  This group of SWWJ members attended the Swanwick Summer School in 2008. (See page 52)

6 The stately old New Cavendish Club, the venue for so many wonderful occasions. (See page 39)

7 The Society has often met in the beautiful Stationers' Hall in London. Vice-President Valerie Dunmore (third from left) joined the Master of the Worshipful Company of Stationers and Newspaper Makers, John Waterlow, and Mrs Camilla Waterlow, together with the Past Master and now Court Assistant Bob Russell at a glittering 'Stationers' evening in January 2008. (See page 22)

8 Princess Diana drops in for tea. (Photograph courtesy of Ann Hancox) (See page 98)

9   Elizabeth Wallace, author and broadcaster living in Denver, Colorado, USA. (See page 39)

10 Edwina Currie MP helps members celebrate the 100th birthday in 1994. (See page 100)

11 From left to right: Sylvia Kent, Christina Adone (*The New Statesman*) and President Nina Bawden at Country Members' Day in 1997. (See page 41)

12 Vice-President Jean Bowden and Honorary Member Jacqueline Wilson, 1990. (Photograph courtesy of Beryl Williams) (See page 118)

# Festival of Britain – 1951

King George VI opened the Royal Festival Hall on 3 May 1951. The Festival of Britain had been organised to mark the centenary of Prince Albert's Great Exhibition of 1851. Elizabeth Harvey was then Chairman. Fortunately, she was also the Press Officer on the official festival staff, her special interest being women's interests and magazines. Elizabeth had managed to arrange a Society tour of the South Bank site in November of the previous year.

Elizabeth later described aspects of her work and of that special time.

> Cheering and flag-waving crowds lined the route taken by the King and Queen to St Paul's from Buckingham Palace. At Temple Bar the procession stopped for a traditional ceremony in which the King was offered the Pearl Sword of the City. The Lord Mayor of London, who enjoys precedence 'of every subject' within the boundaries of the City of London, surrendered his sword, thus indicating the precedence of the Sovereign. The King then returned the sword and the Lord Mayor led the procession on to St Paul's.

Although rationing was still in force, the worst was over, but austerity was still evident. However, the nation's morale was boosted by the Festival. Society journalists covered the event both in national press and in *The Woman Journalist* magazine. The Festival was, of course, celebrated worldwide, giving members the opportunity to meet many of the overseas members who had travelled to London to experience this once-in-a-lifetime event.

# Queen Elizabeth's Coronation

The Loyal Toast to new HRH Queen Elizabeth was offered by the then Chairman, Miss Elise Sprott. Stationers' Hall was the venue and the date 11 June 1953 is remembered by many of the members from that time. The Coronation reception was attended by members who had travelled from many parts of Britain, as well as many from overseas. Council had arranged for an impressive parchment to be designed for special delivery to the Queen. This was created by Mrs Allwood. A facsimile of the greeting appeared in the July 1953 edition of *The Woman Journalist*.

# Diamond Jubilee

The jubilee week opened with a Service of Dedication at St Paul's Church, Covent Garden on 28 September 1954. The Sixth Literary Festival Prize-giving was held at the Royal Society's Assembly Hall in Northumberland Avenue the following day. Clemence Dane, who was just entering her tenth year as SWWJ President, presented trophies to the winners of the Festival which had produced almost 1,500 entries within the dozen writing categories. A cocktail party to celebrate the sixtieth anniversary was held at Stationers' Hall and a visit to *The Daily Telegraph* offices in Fleet Street followed. Visitors were able to see the production of next morning's newspaper with a demonstration of the new wireless photography equipment.

## Off to See the Queen

'Hooray! We are going to London to see the Queen!' Pat Garrod, Editor of the 1969 Spring issue of *The Woman Journalist,* echoed the thoughts of more than 500 Society members. The Society was indeed honoured to be able to announce that Her Majesty the Queen had consented to be present at the reception at the House of Lords which Lady Burton had sponsored on 13 March 1969 to celebrate the Society's seventy-fifth anniversary celebrations.

A moving Thanksgiving service was held in St Bride's that Thursday morning, at which President Joyce Grenfell spoke the heartfelt Bidding Prayer. A buffet lunch followed in the Royal Scottish Corporation Hall and then off to the House of Lords for the party in the Cholmondeley Room, alongside the famous Terrace. 'It was the most wonderful day of my life,' said eighty-five-year-old Emily Moore, who had been a member for almost fifty years. And it was a truly marvellous, magical day.

## Wedding Bells

One special celebration of a romantic kind was on the occasion of one of the longest-standing members, Verily Anderson, marrying Paul Paget at St Bartholomew's Church, in London's Smithfield, in August 1971. Paul, a leading architect and surveyor to St Paul's Cathedral, had restored this church. Joyce Grenfell described herself in her own memoir as 'Verily's somewhat mature bridesmaid'. Sir John Betjeman was Paul's best man. Paul had always been a good friend of the Society and had been guest speaker at several lunch-time meetings. He had kindly invited members to his beautiful home in Cloth Fair, London, where Sir John had been his very good friend and neighbour.

## Princess Diana Comes to Tea

It's not every day that a princess drops in. Hampshire member Ann Hancox and her husband, Vic, had cause for celebration when they moved to Shinewater Court, Eastbourne, in 1989. Both are disabled and their home, one of a collection of flats specially adapted for the disabled, with carers on call, was ready for them to move into. Imagine their delight shortly after settling in to find that Princess Diana would be calling on them. After tea, the Princess studied the visitors' book and insisted on signing it. Ann joined the SWWJ in the 1960s when, as a member of the Guiding movement, her leader, Mrs Brimble, asked if she might be interested in joining the Society. Ann loved the excitement of coming up to London, even though wheelchair-bound. She and Vic had already undertaken some hair-raising trips on canal boats, planes and ships.

Jean Bowden curtseys to HRH the Queen in 1969 at the House of Lords. The occasion was the seventy-fifth birthday of the Society.

# Eighty-fifth Anniversary

In autumn 1979, the customary service took place at St Bride's Church, with the prayers spoken by Joyce Grenfell. This was published in *The Woman Journalist*, which looked back to the life and times of the Society's founder, Mr Snell Wood. Also included were details of the newly-discovered archive material that had survived the fire at the Society's previous venue, the Royal Scottish Corporation Hall in Fetter Lane. To recognise this anniversary, the Society's second anthology, *Candles & Lamps*, was published.

# British Woman Writer of the Year

To celebrate their ninety-fifth birthday in 1989, SWWJ members voted Lynda Lee-Potter their 'British Woman Writer of the Year'. As top female columnist and feature writer on the *Daily Mail* for over thirty years, Lynda had become known as the 'First Lady of Fleet Street'. London's Café Royal hosted the party which 200 members and guests attended. Honorary Life President the Countess of Longford introduced Society Patron Sir Tim Rice, who presented an engraved glass bowl to Lynda.

Honorary Member Lynda Lee-Potter at her desk at the *Daily Mail*.

# Centenary Year, 1994

Perhaps the highest point in the Society's long history was 1994 – Centenary year. The Chairman was the indefatigable Mary Rensten, backed by a hard-working Council team. And strong they had to be, with special events planned for every one of those magical twelve months.

Saturday 11 June was the Centenary lunch and award ceremony organised by the North West Group. It was a sparkling affair. The venue was the Hayward Hall at the University of Manchester and Irene Swarbrick and Chris McCallum and their team organised an excellent lunch, which was attended by distinguished guests Dr Dannie Abse, Dr David Hessayon and Lynda O'Byrne, then Fiction Editor of *Bella* magazine.

The Cholmondeley Room at the House of Lords was the setting for the 19 July when Lord and Lady Longford greeted members to celebrate the Society's 100th anniversary. With Kate Adie, Stephanie Cole, Lady Masham, Baroness Flather and everyone present, they remembered their founder, Mr Joseph Snell Wood, and the pioneers.

During that Centenary year, Daphne Moss, Mary Rensten and Jean Bowden 'christened' the Society's newly-installed bench at St Paul's Churchyard, Covent Garden.

The Gala Day at the Café Royal on 3 November 1994 was magnificent. In the company of the President Nina Bawden and Life President Lady Longford, Chairman Mary Rensten gave an inspiring address, welcoming members and guests, in particular the Rt Hon. Edwina Currie MP.

# Outstanding Journalist Award

In October 2005, members and honoured guests gathered at London's Royal Institution of Great Britain Centre for the award ceremony commemorating the life and work of *Daily Mail* journalist, Lynda Lee-Potter, who had died the previous year. Chairman Val Dunmore announced the winner of the 'Most Outstanding Woman Journalist' of the year, Jan Moir, a journalist on *The Daily Telegraph*, who was presented with a pewter trophy designed by Jennifer Kidd. It was a wonderful evening.

# Special Birthday Party

Member Patricia Pound's first visit to the Society was at the birthday party celebration of President Nina Bawden's eightieth birthday:

> It was an honour to meet this lovely lady, survivor of much tragedy in her lifetime who was about to launch her book *Dear Austen* published that year. This was a poignant story, almost

*Above, left* From left to right: Society Presidents Nina Bawden, Mary Rensten, Lady Longford and Lady Williams attend the 1994 Centenary lunch.

*Above, right* Vice-President Mary Rensten with Penny Ryder dressed as 'the Spirit of 1894' and our Life President Lady Longford at the Centenary Lunch.

*Above* Guests of the Society, journalist Kate Adie and actress Stephanie Cole enjoy the company of members at the Centenary celebrations.

*Right* The Centenary cake.

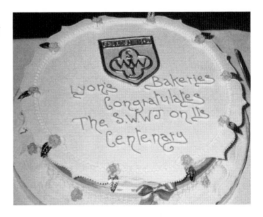

Members celebrate Nina Bawden's eightieth birthday party with ninety-four-year-old Norman Gunby, the historian.

a love letter, addressed to her beloved husband, tragically a victim of the Potters Bar train crash in 2002. Nina's friend and fellow Ilfordian, the historian Norman Gunby was there to congratulate her on a most productive life as a writer and as a powerful lobbyist. Her birthday tea was a happy occasion and her time was freely given, without haste to all who spoke with her. For me that afternoon was inspirational and the first of many occasions spent in great company among the members of the SWWJ.

# HRH Princess Michael

4 October 2007 brought Her Royal Highness Princess Michael of Kent to the Autumn Lunch held at the National Liberal Club, which was overflowing with members. The Princess enthralled listeners with her talk about her own history and her writing life. She brought her latest book, *The Serpent and the Moon*, with her and signed copies for members. Associate Member Paul Harris was on photographic duty and many guests had travelled from overseas. The monologue competition winner was Janet Cameron, who was presented with the cup from competition judge, Simon Brett. This was a day of celebration for members and guests.

# Celebrating at St Bride's

Fleet Street became synonymous with the world of journalism, the press and national newspapers. Since 1500, it has been the home of printing and newspaper publishing. Although, since the 1980s, the presses are now silent, it remains an evocative focal point for all who love the printed word.

Through the years, St Bride's Church has hosted weddings, baptisms and memorial services for the people who had worked in and around the old Fleet Street, including several Society members, some of whom had been regular worshippers.

In December 1940, a wartime bomb shattered this lovely building and for seventeen years, Fleet Street had only the use of a makeshift building. But there was a dramatic reward for this deprivation. For restoration meant excavation, and this gave the archaeologists the chance to explore. As a result of their efforts, nearly 1,000 years were added to St Bride's known history.

In the Spring 1958 edition of *The Woman Writer,* Alex Colbrook, the Society Treasurer wrote:

St Bride's Church is restored after its battering in the war. Its beauty must surely arouse in every journalist feelings of awe and pride that this is the professional's own church. On either side of the central aisle are stalls. These bear plaques of unpolished ebony on which are engraved the names of distinguished journalists and publishers whose memories are still green in Fleet Street. Yet so far, women writers are not represented in this church.

Princess Michael was a welcome guest at the luncheon and prize-giving at the National Liberal Club in October 2007. Janet Cameron won first prize for her winning monologue.

That same year the situation changed. The Society received an invitation asking if they would like to be represented in the form of a stall at St Bride's. They quickly responded and the emblem chosen consisted of the letters in gold, SWWJ on a blue background in a gothic design – the title of the Society and the date of origin – with 1894 in white letters on black polished ebony. Since that date, many members have visited St Bride's to take a look at 'our' stall.

Past Rector of St Bride's, the late Prebendary Dewi Morgan, was a good friend to the Society from the time he arrived to take his up his post in 1962, until his retirement in 1984. His successor, Canon John Oates, also supported the Society in every possible way and was made an Honorary Member, officiating at the Centenary service in 1994 and at other important anniversary celebrations. The present incumbent is the Rector David Meara and Society friendship with this famous church continues.

# sixteen

# *Society Pioneers*

We all need friends. It's true to say that without the fellowship and support of the early members, the Society would not have flourished for more than a century. Space does not allow mention of all its earliest champions, but suffice to mention just a few. Many of the following became members, supporters and even Honorary Life Presidents, drawn from many literary fields.

## Ruby Ayres (1883-1955)

Mildred Pocock, professional name Ruby M. Ayres, joined the Society in 1935. A prolific novelist, many of her books were adapted for films. She was a humorous speaker and one of her most memorable maxims was 'First I fix the price – then I fix the title – then I write the book!' Her first novel, *Richard Chatterton VC,* was published when she was twenty-five. This sold in huge numbers. During a writing life of fifty years she published more than 150 books, at times producing 20,000 words a day.

## Dr Phyllis Bentley (1894-1977)

From 1971 until her death, Phyllis Bentley was the Society's Honorary Life President, following her lifelong friend, Vera Brittain. She was a wonderful writer and author of more than twenty-five novels, set mostly against the background of the West Riding of Yorkshire. Her children's books, based on the textile trade, were popular both in England and America. She was an authority on the Brontë family. Her friend, Mary Howard, wrote in her obituary for *The Woman Journalist,* 'She was the quintessence of all the best things in Yorkshire, perhaps in England.' Mary's favourite of all her books was *A Modern Tragedy.*

## Mary Frances Billington (1862-1925)

Mary was one of the most famous media women of her time. She was President of the Society from 1913-19. Born at Chalbury Rectory, she was daughter and granddaughter of the clergy. From her earliest days, she loved travelling and this is listed in *Who's Who* as her hobby as well as her life work. She began her career with *The Echo,* before becoming exclusively attached to the permanent staff of *The Daily Telegraph,* where she worked as a special correspondent. She is famous for being the only specially invited woman present at the Imperial Press Conference in Ottawa in 1920, representing the Society. Mary made two extensive visits to Nepal, travelling to the North-West Frontier. Her much acclaimed *Woman in India* was a best-seller and, for most of her life her work, particularly the *Red Cross in War,* written as part of *The Daily Telegraph* series of War Books, was published in many editions.

### Marjorie Bowen (1886-1952)

In the days when pen names were often used by well-known writers, member Gabrielle Margaret Vere Long used at least ten. Joseph Shearing was, perhaps, the best known of her pseudonyms. She was a prolific author with more than 150 books credited to her. Marjorie's historical novels were usually based on actual criminal cases. Her true identity was a closely-guarded secret until shortly before her death. Her books had a huge revival in the '60s and are still sought-after works.

### Vera Brittain (1893-1970)

Vera Brittain, described as a feminist and pacifist, was a superb writer and orator and a fighter for the cause of humanity and women's rights. She is well remembered as the author of her unforgettable memoir *Testament of Youth,* which alongside *Testament of Friendship* and *Testament of Experience* are never out of print. Vera Brittain joined the Society in 1943. In 1947, she told a gathering that her family had regarded her writing ambitions as 'merely stupid', urging them to pursue their careers in the face of opposition. She was Vice-President from 1958-65 and succeeded Clemence Dane as Honorary Life President from 1965-70.

### Dame Alida Brittain (1870-1943)

To Dame Alida Brittain, we owe a great debt. She was a journalist, composer, harpist and a distinguished musician. From the time she was elected Chairman on 3 July 1921, she offered support in every way and the Society prospered. Following her appointment as President in 1929, she introduced her husband, Sir Harry, into the Society, who upon her death in 1943 became one of the Society's most loyal Patrons.

Lady Alida Brittain.

### Sir Harry Brittain (1873-1974)

Although Sir Harry Brittain was associated with the Society since its earliest days, it was after the death of his first wife, Lady Alida, that he became a treasured Patron. Born in 1873, his writing skill, energy and personality were such that great honours were bestowed on him. Sir Harry tried to foster closer Anglo-American relations. To this end, he founded the Pilgrims Society in 1903. For seventeen years, first as Honorary Secretary and then as Chairman, he steered them through its early life. He resigned the Chairmanship in 1918 because of his Parliamentary duties, and became its senior Vice-President and then Pilgrim Emeritus. Sir Harry was awarded honorary life membership of the American Club and the Society of Americans in London.

SIR HARRY BRITTAIN — Barrister, Parliamentarian, Writer, Businessman, Traveller, Newspaperman, Founder of Commonwealth Press Union, Winner of the Astor Award 1973

In retrospect – Sir Harry Brittain, our 'constant' caring Patron. (Photograph courtesy of The London Press Club)

On 25 January 1972, Sir Harry was the Guest of Honour at a dinner to celebrate the seventieth anniversary of the Pilgrim Society, at which was read a message from HRH Queen Elizabeth II and a personal letter to Sir Harry from President Nixon. In 1947, Sir Harry donated the Brittain Trophy for the first Literary Festival, and a scholarship in Sir Harry's memory is awarded in alternate years for the Weekend Conference. His achievements listed within *The Times* obituary and *Who's Who* leave the reader impressed that one man could achieve so much in a life spanning 101 years. It was through his love for the Society and wonderful support that we today enjoy strong fellowship with the London Press Club. Sir Harry's second wife, Muriel, supported him and was also a wonderful friend to the SWWJ and attended many special luncheons and celebrations.

### Mrs Colin Campbell (1853-1911)

Mrs Campbell was one of the earliest Council members who cared much about women's rights. She wrote an historic pamphlet that gives us an indication of the difficulties that female journalists were encountering at the end of the nineteenth century. Even today, her words seem strangely familiar. It was said at the time that 'Lady Campbell's cleverness had for several years made her celebrated among London journalists, while her beauty and her costumes are quite as much noticed as when she was merely a member of British aristocratic society.'

### Lady Georgina Coleridge (1916-2003)

Lady Georgina was a good friend and Patron for many years. The world of horse racing was of huge interest to Lady Georgina, as can be seen from her memoir, *That's Racing*. She edited the magazine *Homes and Gardens* from 1947-63. In 1955, Lady Georgina, along with wartime heroine Odette Hallowes and Antonella, Marchioness of Lothian, set up the Women of the Year Lunch Award, which was originally intended as an early attempt at networking. Lady G (as she liked to be called) became President of the Women's Press Club.

### Pearl Craigie (1867-1906)

Mrs Pearl Craigie became the Society's first President in 1894. Through Mr Snell Wood's connection with American journals, it is known that he was keen to recruit this literary star of the 1890s. Born Pearl Richards in Chelsea, Massachusetts, her family had moved from America to England shortly after her birth. Pearl was educated at a boarding school in Newbury, followed by private schools in London. She began writing as a nine-year-old, contributing stories to a newspaper. As was the custom, she adopted the male pseudonym John Oliver Hobbes. At twenty, she married Reginald Walpole Craigie and a son was born, but the marriage was unhappy. Just after the Society of Women Journalists was launched, Pearl was granted an acrimonious divorce, amid huge publicity and scandal. She was a prodigious novelist and playwright and her work was eagerly sought. In August 1906 she died suddenly and prematurely of heart failure and was sorely missed by her colleagues.

### Clemence Dane (1888-1965)

Born Winifred Ashton, this dearly loved first Honorary Life President of the Society took her professional pseudonym from the Church of St Clement Dane in London. She was an amazingly creative woman, a playwright, poet, sculptor and actress, and once a member, gave the Society huge support and infected everyone with her enthusiasm for life. Clemence was known to her friends as Winny and although she was considered to be one of London's most successful novelists and playwrights, she was always friendly and approachable. Her play *A Bill of Divorcement* caused a sensation at the time and was later made into a film. She often had a couple of plays running simultaneously in London theatres. One of her best friends was Joyce Grenfell and it is Clemence we thank for introducing her to our Society.

Eileen Elias, past
Chairman

### Eileen Elias (1912-2009)

Eileen, Chairman and Vice President, had been a member of the Society since 1952. She had written from the age of six. Becoming a journalist during her earlier years, she had never stopped writing articles and books, the last of which, *Victorian Quartet*, was well received. Eileen has had numerous books published to great acclaim. She remarried for the second time at ninety, just as her new book was being launched. Eileen was a mainstay of the Society, serving on the Council in every position over many years, the last of which was Welfare Officer.

### Madame Sarah Grand (1854-1943)

Mrs Sarah McFall was one of the true pioneers of the Society at the end of the nineteenth century. Married at sixteen, she left her husband to become Madame Sarah Grand, a writer of 'indelicate' novels which, nevertheless, sold immediately to the Victorian readers. Sarah was lionised as a novelist, lecturer, Suffragette and defender of 'Rational Dress'. Maybe Sarah was the first feminist. She stressed the need for women to gain knowledge, a sense of purpose and freedom of choice. She truly reflected the turmoil of her age. She became Mayor of Bath and a doughty fighter for women's independence. It was Sarah who coined the phrase the 'New Woman' and seems to have led a colourful life at the end of the nineteenth century. Her books *The Heavenly Twins* and *The Beth Book* became best-sellers.

## Marguerite Radclyffe Hall (1880-1943)

The life of member Marguerite Radclyffe Hall, the poet and novelist who became popular during the 1920s, had been widely publicised during her lifetime. A woman before her time, she wrote about lesbianism and caused outrage in 1928 when her book *The Well of Loneliness* was published. The controversy in the press led to the book being banned in England. However, it sold by the million in America. Marguerite continued writing – her later novels did not pursue such controversial themes – and she won several national awards, including the Femina-Vie Heureuse and the James Tait Black Memorial Prize. Radclyffe Hall and her friend, Lady Margot Troubridge (1887-1963), became Patrons and supported the Society during the early 1930s.

## Elizabeth Harvey (1903-85)

The society owes much to Elizabeth Harvey, who joined in 1938. She did not enjoy robust health, but was determined to become a journalist, turning to freelance writing. She became Literary Editor of *The Birmingham Post* and wrote reviews for *The Times* and *The Times Literary Supplement*. Elizabeth was elected Chairman in 1968. She was the Society's representative on the National Book League and Commonwealth Countries League, and held the prestigious position of board member of the Festival of Britain Council in 1951. Elizabeth loved history and had planned, from 1970, to write about the Society's early history, which she had studied for many years, but health problems prevented this.

## Alice Head (1886-1981)

Alice joined the Society during the 1930s. Aged nineteen, she had been interviewed for a post as a shorthand typist at *Country Life*. Her weekly salary was £1. She began working for Lord Alfred Douglas at *The Academy*, a literary weekly, but left in 1909 to work for Sir (later Lord) George Riddell, the director of George Newnes Riddell, who appointed her Editor of the monthly magazine *Woman At Home* at the age of twenty-two. Alice's life was transformed when she met the American publishing magnate William Randolph Hearst in 1917, who offered her the assistant editorship of *Nash's Magazine* at a weekly salary of £10. In 1923, after the launch of the English edition of *Good Housekeeping*, she became Assistant Editor, then Editor in the following year. Managing Editor came next, a position which she held until 1939. In 1942, she became a director of *Country Life*. She retired in 1949.

## Charlotte Eliza Humphry (1851-1925)

Charlotte joined the Society at the same time as the first President, Pearl Craigie, and was elected to the position thereafter. Like her predecessor, she was a prolific writer, contributing regular columns to *Truth Magazine* under the pen name 'Madge'. Charlotte was the daughter of an Irish parson and arrived in London in the 1870s hoping to earn money as a governess or as a fine embroiderer. Initially, she contributed articles to *The Ladies Drawing Room Gazette* and then began writing for *Truth Magazine*, with her regular column entitled 'Girls Gossip'. For twenty years her 'Agony Aunt' column that specialised in etiquette and good manners was famous and was read as much by men as women, for whom it was originally created. The columns were later published separately as reference manuals, which then became the best-sellers *Manners for Men* and *Manners for Women*, both published in 1897.

## The Countess of Longford (1906-2002)

In 1977, Elizabeth Longford accepted the Society's invitation to become their Honorary Life President. She was a distinguished writer and her books on the life of Queen Victoria and Wellington established her among the first rank of biographers. Lady Longford enjoyed a long and happy marriage – they celebrated their sixty-third wedding anniversary on the day of the Society's Centenary in London in 1994. 'Able, articulate and beautiful' were the words once used in describing Lady Longford by a *New York Times* Editor. As well as enjoying a successful journalistic career and her wonderful large family, she was a superb figurehead and a true friend to the Society. After her death in 2002, an annual Poetry Competition was introduced in her memory. Her published autobiography, entitled *The Pebbled Shore,* was published in 1986.

## Penelope Wallace (1923-97)

Joining the Society in 1966, Penny became Chairman in 1982. She took over her father Edgar's literary estate after his death in 1932 and founded the Edgar Wallace Society, which now has worldwide membership. As a past Chairman of the Crime Writers' Association, she organised the first Crime Writers' International Congress. Although women were not admitted to the prestigious Press Club until 1972, when Penny was finally accepted, she went on to become the first woman Chairman. Her father had held that post in 1923. Penny was famous for her short stories, mostly crime with a touch of humour. She was published worldwide.

## Mrs Humphry Ward (1851-1920)

Mary Ward was another popular writer championing the need for higher education for girls. She wrote for *The Times, Pall Mall Magazine,* and *Macmillan's Magazine.* Following her successfully published children's book *Mitty and Olly* in 1881, she began writing adult novels and her first book, *Robert Elsmere*, was an instant best-seller. Her forays into plays, non-fiction books and novels were successful and her output was impressive. She became a close friend of Henry James and a significant public figure in the English literary world. Other novels which have enjoyed late twentieth-century re-publication include *Marcella* (1894) and *Helbeck of Bannisdale* (1898). Her autobiography, *A Writer's Recollections* (1918), is still popular. She enjoyed a huge readership on both sides of the Atlantic, which made her a wealthy woman. In the early years of the 1890s she founded University Hall (later known as the Passmore Edwards Settlement, and then the Mary Ward Centre).

# seventeen

# *Notable Contributors*

### *The SWWJ Council*

Its aim is to encourage literary achievement, uphold professional standards and promote social contact with fellow writers, upholding the dignity and prestige of the profession of writing in every aspect. Jean Morris is our present Chairman. She and her Council members, each of whom has a designated task, offer a warm welcome to every new member.

Members who have made notable contributions in recent years:

### *Patricia Alderman*

Minutes Secretary Pat Alderman has worked in publishing, journalism, PR and teaching. Her short stories and articles appear in numerous magazines and on radio. Twice winner of the SWWJ Theodora Roscoe/Vera Brittain Cup, she has won many national short story competitions. Pat is interested in writing for children and teenagers with two young adult novels published. A qualified EFL teacher, she is a member of the Society for Editors and Proofreaders. In parallel with her writing, Pat works as an editor on scientific and medical texts and edits and advises on children's and young adult fiction. Pat was a past Vice-Chairman of Sutton Writers and Treasurer of the Lay Buddhist Association in Wimbledon.

### *Pamela Birley*

Pamela has served on Council for many years and as Honorary Secretary from 2005. Following a successful career in personnel and administrative management, Pamela, writing as Bradley Bernarde, has written five novels, the most successful being *The Apothecary's Gift* published by Whydown Books. Pamela reviews books, proofreads and her articles and short stories have received awards. Her work has been published in numerous prestigious journals. Pamela is a member of the Society of Authors and PEN, among other organisations.

### *Eve Blizzard*

Eve joined the Society in 1973 and served on Council as Membership Secretary from 1978-88. Eve is a playwright and has had great success with her work. Nancy Smith was the catalyst who introduced Eve to the SWWJ while at Swanwick in 1972. Eve recalls:

*Left* Pat and John Alderman. Pat is Minutes Secretary on Council and her husband, John, is one of our 'Friends of the Society'.

*Right* Hon. Secretary Pamela Birley with Jean Hawkes, who worked so hard on Council as Secretary, Chairman and Vice-President.

At my first Council meeting held in Stationers' Hall, sitting next to Joyce Grenfell, we unwrapped our sandwiches. Joyce leaned over and looked at my sandwiches with interest. When I admitted to bananas her face brightened 'What a lovely choice,' she said. Flattered at her interest, I offered her one. She promptly did the same, confiding her preference for bananas against her beetroot. Joyce always made you feel better for knowing her!

### Jean Bowden

The Society owes so much to Jean, who joined in 1959. A prolific writer, she has produced more than 100 books under at least ten pseudonyms – Belinda Dell, Jocelyn Barry, Avon Curry, Jennifer Blake and of course, probably her most famous, Tessa Barclay. Jean's writing career spans sixty successful years. Now a Vice-President, Jean has been Chairman, Vice-Chairman and, for nearly thirty-five years, ran the excellent Tuesday Workshops which helped so many members on their way to literary success. Born in Edinburgh, Jean was educated at the school on which *The Prime of Miss Jean Broody* was based. She was taught English by the redoubtable 'Miss Brodie' herself – whose real name, by the way, was something else – and who, says Jean was not pleased at the way in which Muriel Spark depicted either her or the school. Jean was Assistant Fiction Editor on *Woman's Own* magazine and was one of the first people to spot the potential of Catherine Cookson, a later SWWJ member. Jean and her colleague, the late Joan Livermore, produced the beautiful booklet for the Society's Centenary year in 1994.

### Alison Chisholm

Living in Southport, Alison trained from 1969 to teach speech and drama. Her first book, *The Craft of Writing Poetry,* published in 1992, was followed by two more, nine poetry collections, a correspondence course and a mini-book of tips on writing poetry. During her twenty-seven years as a creative writing tutor in adult education, she also worked as a poetry consultant for BBC Radio North-West. She gives talks and runs courses, visits schools encouraging children to write poetry and works as distance learning tutor and poetry columnist for the international *Writing Magazine* and *Springboard*. Alison has won many awards for her poetry, the latest of which is the Elizabeth Longford 2009 Poetry Prize.

### Doris Corti

Joining the Society in the 1970s, Doris is a nationally-known poet who has been at the heart of the SWWJ poetry life from her first meeting. A very fine poet herself, she has served on Council as Poetry Advisor since 1986. She has encouraged the Society's poets through regular workshops and her Poetry Forum in *The Woman Writer*. Doris has won many awards for her poetry, but has also written several non-fiction books which have been well received. She was responsible for the first Poetry Course at the Swanwick Summer School and is a regular poetry columnist and tutor for *Writers' News*. She was involved with the much-acclaimed 'Poets in Schools' scheme, organised by the Poetry Society which was sponsored by WHSmith.

### Beryl Cross

Although Beryl was already 'waiting in the wings' as Vice-Chairman in 1996, it was sad when the Chairman, Daphne Moss, died suddenly in July that year. Beryl took over the Chairmanship with assurance and her two years in office were carried on alongside her previous task on Council of organising many interesting visits around London. Beryl's life has been fascinating and her anecdotes relating to the Fabian Society, her time spent at Ruskin College, Oxford, and interesting links with Russia, would make a best-seller. Beryl is a fine poet and several slim volumes of her poetry have been published over the last few years.

### Val Dunmore

Valerie Dunmore, formerly Francis (aka Sophia Daniel), a member since 1981, became Chairman in 2004. Her hugely varied career path covers business, sport and the esoteric. A journalist since 1976, she wrote for equestrian magazines and has published three books. An expert in New Age topics, she now writes regularly for *Prediction* magazine on dream interpretation, often appearing on television and radio. In 1974, she co-founded with Janet Macdonald the Side-Saddle Association, now worldwide. She is the first Olympic level British judge of international freestyle skiing. Upon leaving office in 2008, she became the first SWWJ Vice-President Envoy. She is a member of the Society's Poetry and Drama Groups.

### Joyce Elsden

A member since 1965, Joyce has served on Council for many years. Her love of the classics influenced her

Peter Durrant, Company Secretary of the London Press Club, was guest speaker at London's New Cavendish Club in December 2006. He is pictured with Chairman Jean Morris.

literary short stories and tales for children, which were published in the *Books for Pleasure* series, *London Life* and *John O'London's Weekly*. When living in Steyning, she entertained members in her home, Nash Manor. Magically, she combines her active business life alongside her successful writing career. Many of Joyce's stories were broadcast on Radio Oman and her features in latter years appeared in *Spare Rib* and *Farm Watch*. A former Membership Secretary, she now plans superb biennial trips to France for SWWJ members.

### Pauline Graham

Joining the Society in May 1966, Pauline became Society Treasurer in 1985. She served more than fourteen years on Council and handled the finances with superb skill. Business and writing are linked in Pauline's world. She lived in Cairo during her formative years and, when arriving in England to live, she could speak French and Spanish but little English. She became a translator, studying during the evenings to become a chartered secretary and followed this with an accountancy course, becoming a certified accountant. She began writing a financial column for *Woman's Own* in the 1960s and went on to publish several books. Well travelled, she is the epitome of the immaculate businesswoman. In 1994, she generously sponsored one of the Centenary writing competitions.

### Wendy Hughes

Membership Secretary Wendy Hughes is a prolific author, columnist and the founder of Walton Wordsmiths. She combines this with her invaluable work on behalf of people suffering from Stickler Syndrome, a progressive genetic connective tissue disorder. Wendy suffers from this condition herself. She campaigns, lectures and writes all the literature for this medical charity and is founder of the Stickler Syndrome Support Group. Indefatigable, Wendy has produced twenty-six books, ranging from non-fiction to children's story activity publications. She has contributed features to magazines as diverse as *The Lady*, *Best of British* and *Guiding*, among many others.

*Left* Pauline Graham, Council Treasurer for more than fourteen years, with Lord Longford, husband of our former Life President, Lady Longford.

*Right* Colleen McMath, Trips Organiser, and Wendy Hughes, Membership Secretary.

## Zoe King

Zoe joined in 2001, and was appointed to Council as Secretary in 2002. Her early writing was in journalism, her first piece appearing in *The Daily Mirror* when she was sixteen. She began writing fiction in 1997, soon after setting up Diss Writers, and has won a number of awards for her short stories. Zoe began teaching her own creativity project, *Journeys to Voice*, on the Internet in 2005, and taught briefly on the much-missed 'BBC Get Writing' site. She is now the Society's webmistress, and designs websites for writers, including the Society's own at www.swwj.co.uk. She currently offers editing and critiquing services, and was, until recently, Editor of *Cadenza* magazine for short stories and poetry.

Zoe King became Hon. Secretary in 2002 and is also webmistress. She was made Vice-Chairman in 2009 and takes the Chair in 2011.

## Arda Lacey

Arda joined the Society in 1966 when she was an active freelance journalist on *The Times* and *The Daily Telegraph* and was also Chairman of the London Writer Circle. Her life in China reads like a James Bond film script. Returning to England in 1947, she wrote on many topics, including poetry. She interviewed many distinguished authors, including the novelist L.P. Hartley. Arda remembers being received by LPH wearing comfortable carpet slippers. Four members of her family joined the Society. Arda remembers meeting the President Joyce Grenfell in the ladies room at Country Members' Day. Arda recalls, 'Joyce was in the cloakroom and at our first meeting in the loo, she made a deep curtsey – she did make me laugh!'

## Jennie Lisney

Jennie has been a professional writer for over thirty years, becoming a journalist and editor. She started her own publishing company in 1994 and successfully edited several trade magazines, as well as working as a freelance journalist contributing to national magazines. She has been visiting lecturer to the Swanwick Summer School and has served as Chairman of Council, Editor of *The Woman Writer*, Minutes Secretary and Publicity Officer over thirty years. Jennie is now a Vice-President and the Society's Regional Group organiser. Alongside other Vice-Presidents, she has now become a trustee for the SWWJ Benevolent Fund.

## Chriss McCallum

A Society member for twenty years, Chriss is an enthusiastic member of the North West Group. She has had a dozen books published over the last few years and numerous columns, articles and short stories. She joined Collins (now HarperCollins) in Glasgow in 1954, working in editorial and book production, becoming deputy department head. Chriss is a popular speaker at writing conventions, specialising in helping aspiring writers to become published. Her latest book, *The Beginner's Guide to Getting Published – How to Write for Publication*, is a best-seller.

## Fay Marshall

Fay joined SWWJ in 1988 and was on Council for six years as Poetry Representative. She organised the annual Julia Cairns Competition, serving on the Critique Service panel. Fay is an 'all rounder', having won numerous competitions in poetry, short story, radio plays and journalism. She studied and was awarded her Diploma in Creative Writing in 1997. Her 'how to' articles were collected for the National Association of Writing Groups' Link booklet *Poetry Guidelines* in 2000. She is busy with workshops, poetry events and adjudication. In February 2009, Fay's translation from Russian poetry was broadcast on BBC Radio 4's *Poetry Please.*

## Anna Milford

Anna Milford is a freelance journalist, photographer, author of several non-fiction historical books – and has been a contestant on televison's *Mastermind*. She joined the Society in 1977 and was Chairman of the SWWJ Charitable Trust, set up in memory of Daphne Moss. Her photographs have provided the archives with many fascinating images over thirty years.

She is also a qualified City of London Guide and has, in the past, arranged tours for Society members and guests. Anna has won most of the SWWJ awards, including the open Centenary article competition with 'Totally Immersed in Genealogy' on the Mormons Family History Index and, most recently, the inaugural Irene Swarbrick Salver for a children's short story 'The Magic Paintbox'.

## Jean Morris

Jean became the Chairman in 2008 and retains the post today. From childhood, she had always wanted to 'write books'. Her first success was a school prize for an essay on the life of Marie Curie. Leaving school aged fourteen, she worked for a Birmingham insurance company. In an article published by *Woman's Realm,* she wrote, 'I'd been awarded a grammar school scholarship, but my parents thought further education was a waste of money. In those days, girls married and didn't go out to work or have careers.' In 1957, Jean, her husband and two-year-old daughter went to live in California.

Jean joined DBE (Daughters of the British Empire*),* a charitable organisation founded in 1909 for women from the Commonwealth or of British birth or ancestry. She was elected Regent of the Simi Valley Chapter in 1964/65. This took her into Hollywood, attending many premiers of British films such as *Camelot,* where she rubbed shoulders with celebrities such as Harry Secombe and Richard Harris. In 2004, Jean appeared on three occasions in a mini-documentary on the *Richard & Judy* television programme on 'How to Write a Novel'. She was featured on the front page of *Writers' News.* Her latest novel, entitled *Oak Trees,* was published in 2009. Jean has won the prestigious John Walter Salver twice.

## Joan Moules

As one of the Society's most prolific novelists, Joan Moules' name is well-known as the author of the definitive biography of Gracie Fields. Joan joined the Society in 1964 and her novels, mainly published by Robert Hale, are rarely out of print. Her first published novel was *Strand of Gold,* followed by *Precious Inheritance* (1979), and, in 1980, *Golden Flame* and *Passionate Enchantment.* Since then, there have been nine more novels, and two biographies.

Vice-President Jennie Lisney, Irene
Swarbrick, Lady Ryder and Lady
Longford.

Joan's latest masterpiece is a crime novel entitled *Script for Murder*. Joan is a delightful,
imaginative writer and one who always supports the Society in every possible way.

### Mary Rensten

Mary Rensten, a prolific journalist and playwright, was born in Leicestershire and brought
up in Jamaica. Back in England, after drama school and college she became a teacher,
writing and producing plays for amateur theatre. This led to her writing for the amateur
and then the professional stage, and for radio. She joined the SWWJ in 1976 and Council
in 1987. As Chairman she guided and inspired the Society during its Centenary year in
1994. Now a Vice-President, she continues to write for national publications and also for
the theatre. Her first novel, *Too Strong A Light*, was published in 2009.

### Eileen, Lady Ryder

Lady Ryder, a long-term member and former Chairman of 1985/86 and Vice-President,
specialised in writing books for very young children. The most wonderful tribute was
presented to her on her ninetieth birthday in 1998. Eileen received the distinguished Papal
Order of Dame of St Gregory from the Bishop of Southwark in the Church of St John the
Baptist. This is a personal reward given by the Pope for good works of national recognition.
What a proud day!

### Jean Marian Stevens

Jean celebrates her sixtieth year with the Society in 2010. As Jean Baxter, she was barely
twenty when she won the Marjorie Bowen Cup for her children's story at the 1949 Open
Literary Festival, then again the following year. Music, rhythm and rhyme have always been
part of her life and Jean has written poetry from childhood. She has won the Julia Cairns
Salver several times and her published work encompasses short stories, articles and plays for
both children and adults, but her main love has always been for poetry. Jean has served on
Council from 1980-2000, as Poetry Representative, Chairman (1983-85), Acting Secretary
and Competitions Co-ordinator, becoming a Vice-President in 1990.

# eighteen

# A Changing World

Time changes everything and so it is with the Society. In the few years since the magnificent SWWJ Centenary year celebrations in 1994, huge changes have taken place, including, sadly, the loss of so many much-loved members and supporters, whose names are etched in members' collective memories. Many of the changes are linked to the world of communication. We now embrace all forms of technology for interaction, speed being the watchword.

## Honorary Members

We appreciate the interest and support we receive from our Honorary Members, Lady Antonia Fraser, Anne Fine, Victoria Glendinning, Dame Jacqueline Wilson and Penny Vincenzi.

## Male Associates

While the Society was created with women in mind, over the years, men have been invited to become Patrons or Honorary members. In 2004, the decision was made to admit men to the Society as Associate Members. Stephen Kendall-Lane became the first Male Associate and he received a warm welcome on Country Members' Day that summer. Over the last six years, more men have been welcomed and they have proved of immense help in contributing their expertise in photography and drama.

## London Meetings

Members from past years will recall travelling to London several times each month to attend the Thursday lunchtime meetings with a speaker organised by programme organisers. The young Jacqueline Wilson (now a Dame and an Honorary Member) worked hard, as did Pamela Payne and, later, Judith Spelman. They somehow managed to find a variety

*Left* Council members in 1993.

*Right* The broadcaster and entertainer Ned Sherrin and Lady Ryder at a Weekend School.

of the best speakers from the world of literature, television, press and entertainment. Speakers at Weekend Schools and special events were eclectic and included politicians such as Barbara Castle, Robert Maxwell (then MP), Geoffrey Archer and Ann Widdecombe; from the stage, Virginia McKenna, Dulcie Gray, David Kossoff, Topol, Dora Bryan and Brian Forbes; and from the world of writing, Count Nicolai Tolstoy, P.D. James, Jimmy Perry, Penelope Lively, Martina Cole (now a member) and many more.

Fiction writing workshops, run primarily by Jean Bowden, Edna Burress, Mavis Heath-Miller, Olive McDonald and Joan Livermore, took place at the Royal Scottish Corporation Hall in Fetter Lane. After the 1974 fire, the venue changed to their King Street address. Members enjoyed lunching in Covent Garden before the lecture. But just after the Millennium, attendances at these workshops decreased, due to the threat of terrorist attacks and spiralling rail costs. Various permutations were tried out by Council, but reluctantly they were phased out.

Now, phoenix-like, the workshops have returned, albeit in different forms and, inevitably, in new venues. Over recent years, members have met at The Writers' House in Haydon Street in the City of London.

Martina Cole, one of our newest members.

*Left* Anita Marie Sackett, current Poetry Representative.

*Right* From left to right: Nina Bawden, Lady Longford, Lord Archer and Pamela Payne at Country Members' Day at the Royal Overseas League in May 1998.

The Drama Groups are popular and numbers are growing. Organised by Benita Cullingford and Associate Member Martin Cort, these are well attended. Silja Swaby arranges exciting whole day sessions for aspiring novelists; Wendy Hughes oversees the successful, buzzing Journalists' Workshops and Doris Corti and Poetry Representative Anita Marie Sackett co-ordinate the successful all-day poetry sessions. Latest workshops concentrate on the short story under the direction of Zoe King.

## Celebrations Through the Year

The long-standing trio of major calendar events through the year start in June with the Summer Festival (once known as Country Members' Day) at which the AGM takes place, followed by the Autumn Lunch, and finally the Christmas Party, all held in prestigious London venues such as the Royal Institution of Great Britain, the Royal Overseas League and of course, the New Cavendish Club near London's Marble Arch.

## Visits

Every two years, a French trip is organised by Joyce Elsden. Regular outings in and around London are arranged by Colleen McMath. These are often behind-the-scenes at theatres, visits to specialist libraries and London museums, and the Trooping of the Colour.

# Weekend Conferences

The biennial residential Weekend Conference, featuring talks, discussions and seminars on a variety of topics, continues to attract many members. These are invariably held at the larger universities around England and have become very special.

# Benefits

Benefits to new members cover the above, details of which are outlined in *The Woman Writer* edited by Penny Legg and issued five times yearly. Here too are regular helpful articles on the creation of websites and blogs, new markets for journalists and a press card, a useful adjunct for researching, particularly in picture galleries. We appreciate the constant flow of online markets and useful writing information from Yorkshire member Jean Currie on the email loop. Also available is a Critique Service and Affiliation Corporate Membership to some of London's clubs and societies.

# Joyce Grenfell

Next year will have significance for all Society members. 10 February 2010 marks the centenary of the birth of Joyce Grenfell. We will celebrate her life and times. Appropriately, we will be holding the Weekend Conference on 24-26 September 2010 at Joyce's favourite college, Lucy Cavendish at Cambridge University, where Joyce was an Honorary Fellow.

Today the Society of Women Writers & Journalists is thriving and is very cosmopolitan. Built on such solid foundations, it has moved into the new Millennium, providing its members with every opportunity to achieve publication, be it in hard copy or electronically.

Our comprehensive website, www.swwj.co.uk epitomises the changing world of the twenty-first century. Our journal, *The Woman Writer,* has increased in size from a simple sheet to a twenty-four-page magazine crammed with exciting news. We are attracting interest from the younger generation and membership is increasing all the time. Our founder, Mr Snell Wood, would be proud of us and pleased to know that his faith in women writers was truly justified.

Chairman Jean Morris with new member Samantha Pearce at the Weekend Seminar in Chester in 2008.

# Bibliography

Bawden, Nina, *Dear Austen,* 2005 (Virago).

Bawden, Nina, *In my Own Time,* 1994 (Virago).

Bishop, Alan (ed.), *Vera Brittain: Chronicle of Youth – Great War Diary 1913-1917,* 1981 (Phoenix Press).

Bowden, Jean & Livermore, Joan, *Centenary of The SWWJ Booklet,* 1994.

Bowden, Jean, *Grey Touched with Scarlet: War Experiences of the Army Nursing Sisters,* 1959 (Robert Hale).

Braithwaite, Brian & Barrell, Joan, *The Business of Women's Magazines,* 1988 (Kogan Page).

Brittain, Vera, *Chronicle of Friendship: Diary of the Thirties 1932-1939,* 1986 (Victor Gollancz).

Brittain, Vera, *Testament of Youth,* 2004 (Virago).

Budworth, Julia, *Never Forget – George Frederic Stewart Bowles,* 2001, privately published.

Burniston, Christabel, *Life in a Liberty Bodice,* 2004 (Westbury Publishing).

Campbell-Preston, Dame Frances, *The Rich Spoils of Time,* 2004 (Dovecote Press).

Compton-Burnett, Ivy, *The Last and the First,* 1971 (Victor Gollancz Limited).

Grenfell, Joyce, *In Pleasant Places,* 1979 (MacMillan London).

Grenfell, Joyce, *Joyce Grenfell Requests the Pleasure,* 1976 (MacMillan London).

Griffiths, Dennis, *300 Years of Fleet Street 1702-2002,* 2002 (London Press Club).

Hampton, Janie, *Hats Off, Poems and Drawings,* 2000 (John Murray).

Hampton, Janie, *Joyce & Ginnie – The Letters of Joyce Grenfell & Virginia Graham,* 1997 (Hodder & Stoughton).

Hill, Marion, *Bletchley Park People,* 2004 (Sutton).

Humphry, Mrs, *Manners for Men,* Ward Lock & Co Limited 1897 & 1993 (Pryor Publications).

Humphry, Mrs, *Manners for Women,* Ward Lock & Co Limited 1897 & 1993 (Pryor Publications).

Longford, Lady Elizabeth, *The Pebbled Shore,* 1996 (Sutton Publishing).

Lord, Elizabeth, *Give Me Tomorrow,* 2006 (Piatkus).

Murray, Jenni, *50 Years of British Women,* 2006 (Vermilion Books).

Rice, Tim, *Oh, What a Circus – The Biography,* 2000 (Coronet Books).

Rice, Joan, *Sand in my Shoes,* 2006 (Harper Press).

Roose-Evans, James, *Joyce Grenfell – The Time of my Life,* 1976 (Hodder & Stoughton).

Shone, Lorna F. & Dudley K., *Agnes Elsie Thorpe aka Agnes Herbert,* Privately published.

Tickner, Professor Lisa, *The Spectacle of Women,* 1988 (Hodder & Stoughton).

White, Cynthia, *Women's Magazines 1693-1968,* 1970 (Michael Joseph).

Wintour, Charles, *Rise and Fall of Fleet Street,* 1989 (Hutchinson).

Wynne-Davies, Marion, *Bloomsbury Guide to English Literature,* 1989 (Bloomsbury).

# Index

# Other titles published by The History Press

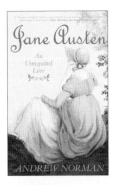

## Jane Austen: An Unrequited Love
ANDREW NORMAN

Jane Austen is regarded as one of the greatest novelists in the English literary canon, and recent film and television adaptations of her works have brought them to a new audience almost two hundred years after her untimely death. Yet much remains unknown about her life, and there is considerable interest in the romantic history of the creator of Elizabeth Bennett and Mr Darcy. Written by a consummate biographer, *Jane Austen: An Unrequited Love* is a must-read for all lovers of the author and her works.

978 0 7524 5529 7

## Chapters in a Mythology: The Poetry of Sylvia Plath
JUDITH KROLL

Judith Kroll presents a study of Plath's poetry, showing that her poems form a mythic biography, presided over by a Moon-Muse, in which depictions of death are nearly always matched with visions of rebirth and transformation. *Chapters in a Mythology* is an original work of fresh scholarship and impressive insight. It remains a compelling examination of one of the twentieth century's great poets.

978 0 7509 4345 1

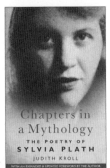

## The Brontës: A Family History
JOHN CANNON

What was the nature of the Brontës' strange genius? Where did it spring from and what inspired it? Patrick Brontë, father of the Brontë sisters, came from Ireland, changing his name from Brunty to Brontë when he won a scholarship to Cambridge. His children never met their Irish relatives and Patrick was deliberately vague about his origins: because of this little has been known about the family's story, which is every bit as strange and romantic as those penned by the sisters in their classic novels.

978 0 7509 4808 1

## Agatha Christie: The Finished Portrait
DR ANDREW NORMAN

When Agatha Christie disappeared from her home in Sunningdale in Berkshire for eleven days on 3 December 1927, the whole nation held its breath. The following day, when her car was found abandoned, a nationwide search was instigated. From a painstaking reconstruction of Agatha's movements and behaviour during those eleven days, Dr Andrew Norman is able to shed new light on what has remained the greatest mystery of all to be associated with Britain's best-loved crime writer, namely that of the woman herself.

978 0 7524 4288 4

Visit our website and discover thousands of other History Press books.

**www.thehistorypress.co.uk**

The History Press